1

THE DOMINO AFFECT
(Reversed)

"THE DOMINO AFFECT"
(Reversed)

A true, untold story of forbidden love, triumph turmoil, and destiny…

The Domino Affect (Reversed)
ISBN 978-0-9975104-0-9
Copyright © 2004 by Karen Domino-White

Cover Design: Karen Domino-White
Rear Cover Artwork: Copyright © 2017 by Karen Domino-White
*Original portrait entitled *"HOT PINK DOMINO"*
Origin of Original Story *(God's Child of Destiny)* – VIRGINIA
BYRD'S LIFE
Editor: Denise Richardson

Printed in the United States of America

Special Thanks from Karen Domino-White to…..

- Charles Amann – *writer, philanthropist, friend*
- Bill Boskent – *producer, writer, confidant*
- Rick Coleman – *author of "Fats Domino and the Lost Dawn of Rock-n-Roll," confidant*
- Billy Diamond – *band leader, bass player, road manager, (jack of all trades)*
- Bernard Dunn – *chauffer for Fats (Virginia's confidant)*
- Reggie Hall – *New Orleans musician, Fats brother-in-law, road manager, confidant to Karen, Veron, and Anton.*
- Herb Hardesty *(1925 – 2016) – saxophonist, trumpeter, song writer, worked with Fats from 1948*
- Denise Richardson – *editor of "The Domino Affect"*
- Elmer Smith – *former columnist for The Philadelphia Daily News*

~*To My Family*~
Maurice White – my husband

Julia – sister	Soyica – son
Cheryl – sister	Lateef – son
Anton – brother	Keira – daughter
Veron – brother	Imani – granddaughter

Barbara "BJ" Johnson *(Aunt Barb) (mom's road dog)*

Uncle Pres *(mom's brother)*
And all my personal friends for all your support!!

Dedicated to my husband, Ted, my parents, my brother Billy.

All of my inspirational friends and family who helped me through many and all of my trials. A special thanks to my brothers Billy, Preston, and Clarence…and my two sisters Barbara and Ann. Most of all my Lord and Savior, Jesus Christ, to whom I came to know as the "Friend of friends."

*Love,
Virginia Byrd*

~My Journey with Fats Domino~

By

Virginia M. Byrd

&

Karen Domino-White

FOREWORD

Destiny, according to Webster's dictionary, is a predetermined course of events, fate; or one's lot in life. When I thought of this definition in relation to my life, I saw in my mind, myself, as a vagabond, walking along a dark, crowded, broad road. At first, I seemed to know my destination, but as I continued, I appeared to be wandering. I stopped suddenly and took out an old worn out road map. It was so ragged that I could not read it. I threw it on the ground and kept on walking lackadaisically. I had gone about one mile when I came upon two large neon road signs. One sign read – *KEEP STRAIGHT AHEAD———TURN RIGHT—>*; the other sign *DETOUR TO ANYWHERE———TURN LEFT*. I paused, read both signs, made a left turn and continued my journey.

I envisioned my destiny as the road to life or death. Not as in physical death, but the emphasis being on how important it is for us to take heed to where we are headed in this life. Understanding that….you can be alive, but not living. Are we on the narrow road that leads to life or on the broad road that leads to possible destruction and failure? How many of us are still taking detours even though the signs are right in front of us.

If we would pay closer attention, we would notice that clearly, all roads are not alike. They are crooked and straight; flat and hilly; smooth and rough; new and old, as well as made of different kinds of materials; such as cement, gravel, tar, and stones. Some roads have signs, lights, arrows, and barrels that warns us of possible danger spots and road construction. Some have bridges that have to be crossed. Others, especially country roads, gives no indication of what is ahead. We begin to travel at our own risk. It becomes imperative that we pay attention to where we are headed.

Several times we ride along talking or listening to the radio, not noticing the road signs, and miss an important turn. We may end up going miles out of the way. Sometimes it is necessary to turn around and go back to our exit. Other times we pull into a nearby gas station and ask the attendant how to get to this highway or that street. The answer may sound something like this, *"Oh yes, go down Main Street to the first stop light, then turn left on South Somewhere Street; go to the third stop light and make a right turn, it will take you right there."* We reply with a thank you only to find out that we may still end up miles in the wrong direction. Do we really listen?

This taught me a very important lesson, that is, *something (or someone) is always sending us a message!* Simple, huh? If only we would listen. Well, like a road, life also has numerous experiences, situations, problems, and circumstances which demand clear-headedness on our part. We have got be willing to be guided whether right or wrong. We can choose to be rebellious, and find answers from the wrong sources, which always takes longer to find the right way.

I have read many memoirs and books on the lives of others. Some have given specific reasons for their downfalls, failures, and disappointments. Their circumstances may vary from child abuse, broken homes, poverty, lack of education; to racial and cultural depravity, with a host of other things too numerous to mention. Others have been quick to put the blame on parents and society. This is not my intention. I say boldly, I do not accept the premise that my race, background, society or any such thing caused me to make my particular choices. I do say that inside, we all get soft, yet gentle, warnings. Some may call it fate, causing many a life to be different had we listened to that voice. But it is O-kay!!!! It's a part of the "Big Picture," my life and your life.

The fact is many, "good people," get side-tracked. Many have strayed off the road of life and become stuck in the mud, many are temporarily off course. Yes, they are still on the road, but have lost the view of their destination. Some are simply fascinated by detours, thinking that they will find short cuts along the way. Temptation knows where we live. If we take heed, our feet will stumble and eventually fall out of the way. Our goal should be to stay on the right path along the way, (as well as we know how), to finish our course.

This testimonial is an account of the many detours I have taken over the years. *"Right when the turns seemed wrong, and wrong when the turns seemed right."* Having said that, we need to recognize and acknowledge that there is always some wonderful good that comes from the choices we make. Even in the worse situations that we find ourselves in, there is some good in them! To live the rest our lives in shameful regrets and total guilt over things that have happened is totally useless. No one can live like that. Ask yourself *"Am I living or just existing?"* I know you may have heard that before but have you answered the question? You may as well never change if your thoughts are still in the past! It's all a part of *YOU* and your life's journey. So embrace all of you, let it go, and move forward knowing that all these things have made you the woman or man you are today. A pie that sits on the table, eventually gets eaten. In other words, as long as you're not standing still but moving forward towards what we know to be right, chances of being devoured by life, are less. Not that everything will be perfect, but the likelihood of disaster is generally less. Nothing can hold you unless *YOU* let it. ***LET IT BE!*** We cannot change the past. Let the past change *YOU*, not own you.

Doing the same things yet expecting

different results is **INSANE**. Allow that light or awakening that's in you, to direct your path and order your steps along life's highway to your beautiful destiny because we all have a "Divine Purpose!" Remember, there will never be another you! Just a little something I've learned, on this long journey of life.

Virginia Byrd

DOMINO EFFECT- DEFINED

As I began to sort out and research the words *"Domino"* and *"Affect,"* I found that the word *"Domino"* refers to a game with worldly recognition, however I noticed that it also is describe as a large loose cloak, usually hooded, worn with a small mask, as to masquerade. The word *"Affect"* is the idea that some change, though small in itself, will cause a similar change nearby which then will cause another similar change and so on, in linear sequence. Like an analogy of a falling row of *"dominoes,"* standing on end.........Just as doing certain things can *"affect"* the heart. . .

I thought that this was very interesting, especially, the word *mask*. I find that we as people, just being the human beings that we are, through natural circumstances, generational issues, and idiosyncrasies, tend to hide who, what and why we are, under a mask of some sort. We take the time to mold, shape, and form our outward appearance to the point of conforming ourselves into the thing that we feel we need to be perceived by others......... Why? Is that really living? So therefore, we all live or have lived with our own personal *"DOMINO-AFFECT"*..... just because the dominoes may fall, does not mean they have to stay down. We all can get up. We have to.........

After my mom wrote this manuscript, she gave it to me and said *"I want you to do something great with this."* At the time I didn't realize the treasure given to me, but after reading I saw her heart on paper. This is her untold story from her womanly perspective. Please read and be blessed.

Karen Domino White

Here's how it starts........

The Domino Affect......

Introduction

SIMPLE BEGINNINGS

Born in Feb 1928, who would believe a young, shy, Antoine Domino would grow up to be one the of the biggest rock-n-roll superstars of the 1950's into the1970's. To date, his music has sold over 110 Million albums and his songs are played multiple times per day, every day, all over the world. Call it fate or call it destiny, some things were just meant to be..

Who would guess that some years later love would raise its beautiful face again in the form of a casual meeting in a local nightclub, down on the Eastern Shore of Maryland. She was a beautiful country girl, some years younger than he. Passion, would merge two hearts together on one cold February night in 1954. Ironically that was the same month Antoine, known as Fats, was born. "Happy Birthday, Mr. Domino....." As forbidden as it was....heart strings were pulled beyond belief, and at what cost? Everything cost something, now........or later. While his music played and climbed the charts.....so did he....so did they...

PART ONE

THE EARLY YEARS

Virginia Byrd

~*My Parents, Birth And Hometown*~

CHAPTER 1

My father, Hilary Charles Polk, the son of Lottie Polk; and my mother, Viola Virginia Hutt, the daughter of Will and Sally Hutt; were both born and raised in Somerset County, on the Eastern Shore of Maryland. His people came from a little community near the City of Princess Anne. There were so many Polk's they named it Polk's Road. Her people came from a place called West Post Office, also near Princess Anne.

During the early 1900's most of the colored

children were kept out of school to work on the farm. This was partially true in my parents' case. There were no schools for the colored in their area. Those that got any education were taught in the local church. Mom was blessed to live near the school for white children.

One of the white teachers had to pass through mom's yard to get to school. Mom would talk to her as she passed by. The teacher soon noticed that mom was a bright little girl and gave her several books to read. By the time mom started school, she had read all of the first grade books and was skipped to the second grade. She learned so rapidly that her teacher put her in the class with higher grades. She was able to go the school through the seventh grade.

Daddy's story is somewhat different from moms. He said, *"the only pair of shoes I had were too small, they hurt my feet; so I stayed home most of the time."* He was able to go through to the third grade. They both had to work as they got older, so neither of them finished high school.

They were married in July of 1931. Mom was seventeen and dad was twenty one. Their first home was an old abandoned school that had been used for white children. It is absolutely amazing that they went to school in a church, lived in a school, and that five of their six children became school teachers and one a preacher/pastor. Somehow I am inclined to believe this is destiny to the utmost.

My mother was an extremely industrious woman. She had a will power that enabled her to try desperately to get her children off the farm and educated. It was her initiative that led us to move several times. It did not matter to her as long as the next house was better than the one we had left. She never had second thoughts about working, neither did it matter what kind of work it was; field work, factory, poultry plant, maid, cook; as long as she could make money to help out.

Daddy, well, daddy was just daddy. He loved

his children; however, it was never a great concern of his that we had oil lamps instead of electricity. He was a farmer, at heart, who loved the old fashioned country life. He was not for all of that fancy city living. He was perfectly satisfied wherever we lived, as a matter of fact, even happier if he could plant a garden, build a fence and raise a few chickens.

My parents are now in heaven with the Lord and through all of these years, the one quality I admired in both of them was integrity. They taught us well, and raised us to be responsible, hardworking, God fearing people, even though for many years, they were not even involved with religion that much.

I was born on Independence Day, July 4, 1933 in the City of Salisbury, Wicomico County, Maryland. My parents were still living in Somerset County at a little place called "Palmetto," near Princess Anne. There were no hospitals in Princess Anne, so mom had to go to Salisbury, about twelve miles away.

I was the third of eight children (now the oldest of six). The first two children died, one of pneumonia and the other still born. Mom had planned to spend the 4th of July at Tasley Fair (a town in Virginia) however, she gladly settled for a nine pound bouncing baby girl. I am not sure how much that had to do with her naming me, Virginia. I was the first of their children to survive, hence, destiny was already on my side.

The day I was born, our nation celebrated 157 years of declared independence from England. When I became old enough to understand what they were celebrating, I was flabbergasted at the idea of my country and me having the same birthday. I was even more excited with all of the fireworks, parades, high flying flags, public ceremonies and picnics, all for the two of us. I sensed that there was something special about being born on the 4th of July.

Although the nation was celebrating, we were

going through the worst economic crisis of the century, The Great Depression. Our new President Franklin D. Roosevelt had been in office exactly four months, having been inaugurated March 4, 1933. The famous "100 days" special session was over and Congress had passed New Deal social and economic measures. There was a ray of hope; our chief executive had pledged himself to restore prosperity to the country. Things were beginning to simmer in Europe also; Adolph Hitler had been named Chancellor of the Third Reich in Germany. The powder keg of World War II had been opened and the Chancellor had the match in his hand, waiting to strike it.

By the 1930's hard times had set in, especially for the people on the Eastern Shore. Daddy found work as a tenant farmer or sharecropper. He was provided with credit for seed, tools, living quarters, and food for our family. He worked the land and received an agreed share of the value of the crops minus charges. The disadvantage with this kind of work was that he usually did most of the work and received a meager salary. It amounted to a "dollar a day". This really was not too bad, because we could buy a week's groceries for about $3.00 and still have money left to splurge. A loaf of bread was 5¢, two pounds of sugar was 25¢ and five pounds of flour was 50¢. Clothes were cheap then; a pair of overalls cost $1.98 and a pair of shoes about $3.00. Mom bought a brand new spring coat for $5.00. They also ordered clothes from the Spiegel catalog on credit.

This did not last long however, the plight of the farmer got worse. Congress passed the AAA (*Agricultural Adjustment Act*) which assisted mainly the politically powerful farming minority that specialized in commercial crops. It largely ignored the sustenance farmer and severely injured the tenant farmer and the sharecropper, who were moved off the land, withdrawn from production.

Daddy tried to improve his lot by working as a lumber jack, *(a person who cuts down trees and makes them ready for the saw mill)*. Logging was probably next in importance to farming on the Eastern Shore. This was his source of income during the winter months. In addition to working at the saw mills, he also moved from farm to farm. During a period of about ten years we moved to three different farms, owned by Elwood Pusey, Wilmer Adkins, and Fred Hitch.

Fruitland

In 1935 we moved to Fruitland, a little town in Wicomico County about three miles from the county seat, Salisbury. "The town was founded in 1820 and was originally named Forktown because it was located in the forks of the roads. These roads were used by the stage coaches as a thoroughfare, North and South. Forktown, at that time, was a part of Somerset County.

The Stagecoach trail originated in Accomac Virginia and went to Philadelphia, Pennsylvania. At that time, the road was known as Stage Coach Road at Forktown. The Stage Coach stopped at

Forktown, changed horses and went on its way. At this stop was a hostelry, tavern, and stables.

On April 14, 1873, the name of the town was changed to Fruitland, a name derived from, and concurrent to, the large crops of strawberries, blackberries, and other fruits grown and harvested in this location. Part of Somerset County was re-zoned, the northern part which included Fruitland and an area about three miles South of Fruitland were added to the southern part of Wicomico County. Fruitland was incorporated in 1947 and by 1950 had a population of 1,028 people. [3]

A casual stroll down Main Street in Fruitland to the 5¢ & 10¢ store, Post Office and grocery store was a thrill for me. Since I was the oldest child, I had the pleasure of running errands for mom. I particularly enjoyed the trips to Hayman's and Crockett's stores because we had a "store bill" or "charge account" at both places. We could get groceries and pay for them on the weekend or at the end of the month. I had a natural inclination to add such "perishable" items as ice cream on a cone and cold pop to mom's list. We lived about two miles from town, on St. Luke's Road, so all of the "goodies" would be gone by the time I got home. The length of my trip depended on whether or not I saw a dog along the way. I had to pass by the home of the Shores who had several "bad" dogs. One of them, the "big brown one," did not like the looks of me. He would bark when I get near the house, and I would run as fast as I could. He chased me until I found a big stone or something to throw at him. They finally tied him in the back, so that he could not see me as I passed by.

Besides Hayman's and Crockett's, there were several other businesses on Main Street, including Conley's Hardware, The Fire Department, Dr. Daisy's Office, the Bank of Fruitland, Claude Bound's store, the Barber Shop, Smith's Groceries, the Fruitland Shirt Company, John H. Dulany's Canning Company, just off Main, and Monroe Pollits Taxicab stand. Mr. Monroe started his cab business back in 1919, with a Model T-Touring car. On Saturday nights, he made as many as four trips an hour from Fruitland to Salisbury, about three miles. The fare at the beginning was only 10¢. During World War II the fare was raised to 15¢. By the time I turned fifteen, Mr. Monroe had raised the price to 25¢. We teenagers were outraged at the price hike.

To my knowledge there were two white churches on Main Street; St. John's Methodist and the Christian Church. The three colored churches, Mt. Calvary Methodist, Mt. Olive A.M.E., and Rose of Sharon Pentecostal were located in the colored neighborhoods. It always puzzled me how the coloreds and whites lived in separate areas, went to separate churches and schools. As far as I knew, we had separate Gods too.

Since the population was very small, I practically knew all the families of Fruitland, both colored and white. I had several white playmates, but the closest one was Suzie Mezick. I admired her roller skating ability. She tried to teach me to skate; however, I was more interested in playing school. Some of the other white kids were not allowed to play with us colored kids. There were some real nice people in Fruitland, in spite of the few who were extremely prejudiced.

In 1952 or 1953 we moved from the farm down on St. Luke's Road, "up to Fruitland", in our vernacular, that is to say, we moved into the heart of the town. We moved to a tenant house that had once been the town's first Fire Company. The Fruitland Fire Company had been organized in that same building in 1912. We called it the "fire engine house." It was an old dilapidated, two story metal building that had once housed fire trucks. Mom had a semi-nursery on the first floor. We ate and slept on the second floor. One of the problems with this place was that we had to go outside to go upstairs. We got a lot of exercise, running up and down those steps. We had electricity, but no indoor plumbing.

No matter how many problems we encountered or what the attitudes of the people were, I still loved Fruitland and the people who lived there. I went to school there, played and stayed there until we moved to Salisbury in early 1955 or later 1954.

Salisbury, the county seat of Wicomico County was much larger than Fruitland. As a matter of fact, I had often dreamed of living in Salisbury, after all that's where I was born. The population was approximately 15,000 by the 1950's. We were blessed to move into a brand new apartment. This was almost like living in luxury. We had modern conveniences, including a bath tub. This was the beginning of a new era and experience for our family. We said good-bye to that farm and to the "fire engine house."

~*On The Farm*~

CHAPTER 2

My entire childhood was spent on the farm. Daddy raised corn, cucumbers, tomatoes, potatoes, watermelons, cantaloupes and strawberries, and sold them. We also had a big garden every spring. My brother Billy and I were assigned special duties such as hoeing, feeding the chickens, gathering eggs, watering and feeding the pigs, pulling grass out of the crops and at times milking the cow. We also had to help to pick the crops during harvest time.

One of the most vivid memories for me, was the first time I tried to milk the cow. I though old

Betsy was the meanest cow in the world. She swished her tail, kicked, looked around at me and mooed. I was determined to milk her. My efforts were thwarted when she kicked the bucket over several times. When the ordeal was over, I had about one glass of milk. I could imagine what the milk man had gone through to make daily deliveries in the community. After several attempts, I learned how to milk the cow.

Hog killing was a big event at our house. About once a year, usually during the winter, daddy killed the fattest hogs. Some of neighbors always assisted him. I left home and visited my grandparents most of the time, because I felt so sorry for those poor "critters." The sight of all the meat and the smell of making lard made me sick. It was quite a while after hog killing before I ate fresh sausage and ham. I threw most of it under the table to our cats. I got used to it as I got older, but even now I still have no desire to eat "hog chitterlings."

Billy and I had a lot of sympathy for the animals, especially for our pets. We once had a funeral for our pet dog. He preached the sermon and I sang songs. We buried him and put a stick marker on the grave. It was even hard for me to kill chickens. I once took an axe and cut a chicken's head off. It ran after me for a long time with no head. I ran into the house, closed the door and waited until it died. That was my first and last time of cutting off a chicken's head with an axe. We had so many animals that our farm looked like Old MacDonald's. All the animals, the cows, mules, horses, pigs, cats, dogs, chickens, ducks, and goats, were our personal friends. I was hurt when they were hurt and sick when they were sick.

For several years, there were only two children in our family. Barbara, Preston, Clarence and Anna came later. Daddy's sister, Aunt Evelyn had two children, Sophie and Harold, who were just about our ages. I was four months older than Sophie and Billy was about a month younger than Harold. They were our playmates; however, at times we were rivals. Sophie and I had a big fight because she tore the flowers off my new hat. I do not remember who won; she probably did, because I was devastated over my new hat. We later became very close friends and in time, became the neighborhood bullies. Sophie and I could beat all the kids in our area. We stayed with her a lot because Aunt Evelyn treated us like her own children. She brought us the same things she did for Sophie and Harold, she also gave us all money to buy "goodies" from the store.

Billy and Harold did not fight each other too often, but they did a lot of foolish things, like letting their goat out into the neighbor's fields. This prank soon led to serious consequences, especially when they let the goat eat up Mr. Walter White's crop. What a scare they had when he came to our parents about their actions. Somehow they managed to lie out of a whipping, but had to get rid of the goat.

My brother and I also got into a lot of

mischief. We were playing one day and I broke the lamp chimney. We used old fashioned coal oil lamps with glass shades called chimneys. After I had broken the glass, I ran out to the field and told daddy that Billy had broken it. He said, "OK, I'll take care of him when I get to the house. Get me a switch." I ran back and told Billy, "You gonna' get a beating, just wait till Hilary gets home." I used to call my daddy, Hilary. Well, daddy came to the house and asked for the switch. The nice, long, limber switch that I had gotten for Billy. As I handed the switch to him, he grabbed me and gave me a good whipping, and then Billy got his. My, how surprised I was to learn that daddy had not believed my, well, call it what it was, a fabrication! He knew that I had lied. I know now what Solomon meant when he wrote, "foolishness is bound in the heart of a child, but the rod of correction shall drive it far from him." (Proverbs 22:15). Daddy used the rod well and I learned a real lesson on telling the truth.

Billy and I had one adventure that has helped

me to avoid smoking cigarettes. Daddy's favorite brand was Chesterfields. We decided to try them out one day along with his Prince Albert chewing tobacco. We waited until our parents had gone to the field for the morning, and then got the chewing tobacco and cigarettes. I climbed up to the cabinet and took out the box of matches. We were all set for the great experiment. I lit up first, then handed Billy a cigarette. We smoked almost a whole pack of Chesterfields and chewed a plug of tobacco. We must have picked the hottest day of the summer, because the heat and tobacco combined made us drunk. We got so sick that we had to go outside for fresh air. The coolest place was under a shade tree. We managed to rest under the tree until mom and daddy came in for lunch.

They soon realized that something was wrong when they saw us there under the tree, but they did not know what was going on. At first they thought we had accidentally eaten some pesticide or spoiled food. The truth came to light when I tried to tell them what had happened, holding my hand over my mouth. I couldn't hold it in very long. It all came out in a big "gush" in my mother's face. Ah! Then they knew we had been chewing tobacco and smoking. They started to whip us, but finally decided that we had been punished enough and had learned our lesson. This was true in my case, because I have not smoked another cigarette or used tobacco in any form since that day.

Even though we were little rascals at times, there were some very pleasant times on the farm. I have many unforgettable memories of working for Mrs. Sarah Sermon, our white neighbor. She was about seventy years old, and very wise. I helped her to pick vegetables from the garden, clean the house, and gather eggs. Mom sent us to her often for milk and eggs when we ran short.

Mrs. Sermon lived in an old fashioned farm house with beautiful furniture that would now be considered antique. My favorite was a wicker rocking chair, just about big enough for me.

She had a special love for children. It did not

matter to her that we were little colored children. Mrs. Sermon took a special interest in my school work. She allowed me to read a lot of her books and magazines. Now and then, she would allow me to take them home to read, and then return them when I finished. I remember sitting on the stair steps in her kitchen, watching as she baked cookies, cakes, biscuits and pies. I was her official taster, so I tested them as she took them out of the oven. They were good. I also got a big kick out of answering the telephone for her. She had one of those old crank up styles that hung on the wall, with a bell on the outside. Stella, the operator, knew each family on the line personally. I enjoyed talking to her. I learned an important lesson, while working for Mrs. Sermon, that is, that love transcends all barriers, especially color. I loved her and could feel her love for me.

As I recall those early years, I suppose my greatest achievement came in taking care of my little brothers and sisters. Daddy and mommy gave me special permission to do whatever was necessary, even whipping them. Those were very precious and formative years for me; however, my brothers and sisters views may be quite different from mine. To them I was the big sister, with the big stick. They were the sweetest, naughtiest, little rascals to be found anywhere. Barbara and Preston kept me very busy. Barbara was a very creative, inquisitive child. Sherlock Holmes, Perry Mason, Tom Sawyer and Huckleberry Finn, did not have anything on her. She could invent, devise, and imagine things to do or get into. She could also find anything that was hidden. I once hid some dried peaches in the pantry to cook for dinner, so I thought. Barbara found them and the two of them devoured my peaches. Poor Preston! He always got caught following Barbara. As soon as I discovered my loss, I asked, "Who ate the peaches?" They did not know. When I got the switch, Preston said his favorite words, *"Oh, Ginyer's gonna' beat us Barber, you go first."* He had big bright eyes that seemed to sparkle and dilate when he thought he was going to get a whipping.

Clarence and Ann had somewhat different personalities. They were both very sick as youngsters, so I had to be extremely careful with them. Then too, they were normal little kids compared to Barbara and Preston. I think they took heed when they saw Barbara and Preston get the switch. At times Clarence thought I was a tyrant who needed to be dethroned. He tried a coup d'état when he was in high school. It didn't work, I whipped him. I enjoyed taking care of all of them; I gained some very helpful experience that came in handy later as my own children were born.

Those adventurous, fun filled days in the rural area made a life-long impact on me. The countryside with its wide open spaces, the smell of pine trees and wild flowers, the walks down those long dirt roads in route to the fields, the excitement of roaming through the woods with an occasional stop to pick wild huckleberries, have all been unforgettable. I have been unable to find anything more relaxing than lying in the backyard, on a cool summer evening, about the edge of dark, imitating bob-whites and whippoorwills. That impression has been so lasting that even now, I whistle when I am happy. I thank God for such a fruitful background on the farm.

~My Grandparents~

CHAPTER 3

At Lot's House

On weekends Sophie, Harold, Billy and I stayed at daddy's mother's house. We called her Lot, but her real name was Lottie Polk. She was the daughter of Henry and Amanda Polk of Folk's Road, Somerset County. Amanda was a Cherokee Indian. Lot was a short; heavy set, brown complexioned woman, with high cheekbones and straight long black hair that attested to her Indian heritage. She was a sweet, mild natured, hardworking person. Her main job was maid, cook and housekeeper for several of the prominent white families of Fruitland. She loved her grandchildren. As far as my grandfather, I never heard or knew anything about him.

Lot's house was an old fashioned, wood paneled dwelling, with five rooms and a tin roof. She lived at two or three locations, but the one I remember best was the house on Mr. Elwood Pusey's farm. There was absolutely nothing more fascinating to me than to wake up to the pitter-patter of rain dropping on that tin roof.   The yard was large, with walnut, persimmon, apple, peach, and pear trees in the back. There were also several grape vines.

My father's brother James (Uncle Jamie), my cousins, Pecola and John Ed, and Lot's brother, Uncle Emory lived there also. Uncle Jamie was quite a character. He played with us and gave us money for helping to feed and water the chickens. He raised chickens for sale. He sent us to the store, when all the chores were finished, to buy pop, candy, cookies, and ice cream. He always made certain that we had change to spend on ourselves. Our main stop was Wilson Tarr's store, across the railroad track from Lot's house.   We filled our pockets with penny candy for 25¢.

Lot allowed us to stay up late on Saturday nights while she cooked her Sunday dinner. We listened to WCKY our favorite radio station at that time because they played country music.   Some Saturday nights we listened to Uncle Emory's tall tales. He was very good at telling us Uncle Remus stories and ghost stories.   Many times we were horrified at the thought of going up stairs to bed in the dark after one of Uncle Emory's ghost stories. We used oil lamps that had to be turned down or put out before we went to sleep.   We took turns looking under the beds, checking the closets and the empty room at the end of the hall before we got in bed. We shuddered at any strange noise. Pecola, who was about seven years older than we were, had to stay awake and assure us that everything was alright. Sophie and I stayed close to her at night, but she could not get us to obey her during the day. We thought she was being smart or trying to boss us because she was in high school. We got revenge by looking in her dresser drawer, reading her little "love" notes to and from her boyfriend. We were real scoundrels.

Now, back to Lot, she was an excellent cook. We could always smell the aroma of those delicious apple, sweet potato, and mince meat pies from out in the yard or as we walked near to the house. She usually cooked fried chicken, roast beef and yams, ham, turnip greens, and corn bread. Our uncles, aunts, cousins, neighbors, and friends came from miles away just to eat at her house on Sundays. The guest were always served first, the children last. We used to stick our heads out of the living room door to see if the adults had eaten all of that good food. Lot would say, "Now you children get back in there and wait." Boy, were we glad when our turn came! We had to eat a healthy portion of meat and vegetables before we got to the desserts. Lot seemed to know what each of us liked best. My favorite was homemade vanilla ice cream and coconut cake. We took turns at helping to freeze the ice cream.

I had a great taste for food period. That's another reason I liked to stay at Lot's. During the summer she took us to the Folk's Road and Oaksville Camp meetings. These were annual church camp meetings. People attended those meetings mainly for the food, drinks (all kinds), and the preaching. They also had prayer bands. They set up booths on the church ground and sold food. They sold fried oyster fritters, chicken n' dumplings, fried chicken, sweet potato and apple pies, cornbread, fried fish platters and sandwiches, homemade ice cream, soda pop, fresh lemonade, and watermelon. I ate until I was stuffed. People usually brought ice cream cones to me. They called me "Miss Lot Folk's pretty little granddaughter, just like Miss Lot." This swelled my head. I thought I was the cutest thing at the camp meeting, all dressed in my little white dress, black patent leather slippers, and ribbons on my long plaits.

Those were precious weekends and days at Lot's house. She worked and served her family until sickness over took her. She was bed ridden for more than a year, but she was always happy to see us when we visited her. She died in 1953. That was a very sad day in my life. I will cherish the memories of a loving spirit, life and vitality forever.

Pop Will and Mom Sally

When Billy and I were not at Lot's, we stayed with mom's parents, Will and Sally Hutt; better known as Pop Will and Mom Sally. Mom Sally was born and raised in Somerset County, Maryland. Her parents were Greensbury, (Grandpop Green) and Mary, (Grandmom Mary) Ballard Bivens. Grandpop Green was a slave as a boy and became a local preacher as he grew older. Grandmom Mary was a very popular midwife in Somerset County. The story is that her father Jim Ed Ballard was a white man. I never knew much about Pop

Will's people, but his parents were George and Mary Hutt from Worcester County, near Snow Hill, Maryland.

To my recollection, Pop Will and Mom Sally lived on at least four farms. Most of the happenings went on when they lived on Mr. Carl Bussel's farm, located about ten miles from the town of Fruitland. Their house was very old, probably built during the late 1800's or early 1900's. It had about seven rooms, two porches and a large yard. On any given weekend, there were as many as fifteen to twenty children there. My aunts, uncles, and cousins came by and literally dropped off their children every Saturday night. The older children helped Mom Sally to take care of the younger ones.

Mom Sally was a very unique, special, God fearing woman. Her greatest attribute was her love for people, especially total strangers. Any "hobo," vagabond, or wayfaring person was always welcomed to spend the night at her house and to have a decent meal. She would take the clothes off her back and food from her table to help someone in need. She was also a very talented person, although she never used it very much. I remember listening to her play and sing, *"What a Friend We Have in Jesus,"* and *"Sweet Hour of Prayer"* on an old fashioned peddle organ. I am told that once when her house caught on fire, she ran upstairs, grabbed up a big barrel of flour, and carried it out into the yard, and then could not lift it afterwards.

During the winter Mom Sally made holly wreaths for sale. The holly business was big in Fruitland. Holly buyers say that the Fruitland Auction was the first block in the United States and started in the 1880's. Mom Sally could make up to twenty or more wreaths in an hour, for about 50¢ a piece. Most of the farm women did this for extra money. Pop Will and my Uncles, Joe and William, gathered in the hoops that were used to mold or form the ringed shaped wreaths. The children helped to tie clusters of red berries together, to be wired on the dark green holly leaves. They made beautiful wreaths. These were made about three weeks before Christmas, so Mom and Pop had money for the holidays.

Pop Will was a very unusual grandfather. He taught the girls how to cook and do the house work. My homemade biscuits are the result of his thorough teaching. He stood and watched as I tried to make bread without getting my hands messed up. Then he would say, "Ginny, put your hands in the dough and work it real good, be sure to put enough yeast powder and lard in it." When I obeyed, the bread came out perfect every time, when I didn't, I had to throw it away and start again. After all the cooking was done, he saw to it that we washed the dishes and swept the floors. I think he got a lot of joy out of teaching us girls how to be good housekeepers.

Pop often walked to the country store to buy the "grub" as he called it. What a thrill it was to look out of the window and see him coming down that dirt road with a burlap bag over his shoulder. We watched until he got almost to the house, and then ran out to meet him. We just knew what he had in the bag; flour, coffee, sugar, molasses, beans, fatback, baking powder, and some good ole candy and cookies for us grandchildren. At times he would tease us by taking out the goodies last. We would stand there with our mouths watering and eyes bucked waiting for him to get to the bottom of the bag, then he gave it to us. It was the best candy and cookies in the world and even better because Pop Will brought it for us. He truly loved us, and we knew it and loved him.

When I was about seven years old, I tried my hand at "rubbing snuff" (it is now called dipping), like Pop Will and Mom Sally. I stayed all night and slept at the foot of their bed. Mom Sally kept the snuff box on the table beside the bed. I said to myself, "As soon as they go to sleep I'm gonna get me a rub of snuff." I don't remember what kind it was, but I do remember thinking it was sweet. I waited until I thought they were asleep, and then crawled out of bed, eased to the table quietly, so that I would not arouse them, got the snuff box, opened it, scooped it out with my finger, and filled my lip with my finger as I had seen Mom Sally do. Then I got back into bed and tried to go to sleep. I didn't know you had to keep expectorating, so I swallowed the juice. I got so sick and drunk, that I woke up Pop Will and Mom Sally. I heard Mom Sally say, "Lord Will, this child's tried to rub snuff." I was sick all night, but they stayed up with me and scolded me. I finally got it all out and went to sleep by morning. Now, it is hard for me to imagine why some young people want to dip snuff, however, we all have been curious about many things at one time or another.

Mom and Pop's house was always filled with excitement. We helped to do the work, such as washing dishes, sweeping the floors, feeding chickens and pigs, picking vegetables from the garden and many other chores. I learned how to chop wood and bring it in from the wood pile. Boxing matches were a common sight in the yard. I now call it the *"survival of the fittest."* Not a day passed that some of us didn't get into a fight. We actually tried to see, among the grandchildren, who was the best fighter in the family. It was fun while it lasted, even though we were punished afterwards.

Pop Will once heard me whistling and said, "Ginny stop that whistling, don't you know that a whistling woman and a crowing hen is no good for God nor Man?" I do not know where Pop coined that old saying, but I still think of it when I whistle, and I must say I still love to whistle. Well, Pop became ill and stayed sick for a long time. He died in 1953 after a stroke. Mom Sally at this writing is ninety-nine years old and still full of love and life. She now has a host of grand, great, and great-great-grandchildren. She was so blessed in her own beautiful way. The love, concern, and wisdom shown by them have had a lasting effect on my personality. I thank God for grandparents.

Note: Mom Sally departed this world in 1987 at the age of 105

~*Awareness of God*~

CHAPTER 4

By the time I was eight years old I knew that something deep down inside of me wanted to know about who God was. Where did He live? I had many dreams about this place people called Heaven from the age of five on up. I think it started when I went to my great-grandmother's funeral. This was grandmom Mary, Mom Sally's mother. She looked so real in the casket. I listened as the preacher talked about how she was going to be with God. He said that she was a, *"Child of God."* I decided then that I wanted to be a *"Child of God."* I did not know what that meant, but I knew if I was good I could go to be with God. The thought of being *"God's Child"* remained with me from that time on.

I had a fear of God because I could not understand who He was. Billy and I went to the fields often and walked down the rows behind daddy as he planted the crops. Each time I would look up to the sky I'd ask questions like, "Where is God? What does He look like? Can God see us now? How can God keep those clouds up there without them falling on us?"

My father didn't go to church or anything much then, but he answered my questions the best he could. Those answers did not satisfy my curiosity. I continued to ponder those ideas and questions in my heart. I was afraid to be left alone in the field, but by the age of twelve I enjoyed working in the fields. There was something majestic about the open fields and the smell of the crops and grass. I could sense that a greater power was helping me to pick strawberries, beans, tomatoes, potatoes or whatever I did. I could pick more and work faster than my cousins and friends. No matter what the job was, I did it extremely well and usually made more money than the other kids my age.

Our family went to church on special occasions like funerals, weddings and those old fashioned, outdoor camp meetings during the summer. I remember the prayer bands at those camp meetings. I made it a practice to go near the group, and to listen as they prayed. They got down on their knees in a circle and talked out loud. They were speaking to God, asking Him to bless them and their children. They thanked Him for food, shelter, and clothes. They asked God to bless and anoint their pastor. I was fascinated as I observed their actions; clapping, singing, and even dancing as they got up. To me, they were having a good time with God. I wanted to learn how to talk to Him too, so I imitated what they said and did when I got home to myself.

When I was about six or seven a little old lady came to our house. I am not sure, but I think she was a Jehovah's Witness. She was at least seventy years old and could not hear well. She brought records and played them on a Victrola, one of those old crank up record playing models. Mom would let her in most of the time, but we wouldn't answer the door when we did not want to be bothered. We could look down the road and see her coming in a little rumble seat car. This dear little lady did not allow her handicap to hinder her witnessing. She planted a seed. An awareness of a higher being came in time.

Pop Will and Mom Sally took us grandchildren to church with them often, mostly on Sundays and Sunday nights. It was fun for me, because we had to walk to and from church. We took turns at night, pulling pranks and scaring each other, as we walked in the dark. The children were made to sit in the back of the church. We always found something funny to laugh or snicker at, especially when the adults would shout (or do the holy dance), as it was called. When Mom Sally caught us playing, we had to move up to the front and get down on our knees to pray. At times some of the older saints would anoint us with oil and pray for us.

This Pentecostal group was very legalistic, meaning the women wore long dresses, hats, cotton stockings, and no make-up. They did not press (or straighten) their hair with hot irons, although it was a custom in the colored neighborhood and among the coloreds who were considered worldly. The preacher told us that we needed to give our lives to God. He said, if we didn't we would go to Hell. He pleaded each time we attended. Some of the young people pretended to be saved and I believe some of them opened their hearts. I was not even ready to pretend. I could feel the pressure pulling me to join the church, even though I did not answer the call at that time; goodness answered the prayers of those dear church members.

My parents did not claim to be religious, but

we were taught that Christmas was Jesus' birthday. We looked forward to it every year. I wrote a long list of toys I wanted for Christmas. There was one thing that puzzled me about Christmas, which was how Santa Claus got all mixed up in Jesus' birthday. I thought perhaps he was the errand boy who brought the things that God sent to us.

Christmas was a big time for us. Daddy started admonishing us to be good a month before Christmas day. Once when we were walking home from Grandma Lot's house with him, on Christmas Eve, we heard bells ringing in the distance. I got excited and said, "Oh daddy is that Santa Claus?" He answered, "I bet it is." I ran ahead quickly to get home before Santa Claus got to me. I thought Santa Claus was funny looking. I wanted the toys, but no part of him.

Our Christmas list usually included a wagon, guns and holster, coloring books, crayons, candy and fruit for Billy. A doll, baby carriage, books, blackboard, chalk, candy and fruit for me. As we got older, our list included clothes and essentials, especially after we found out who Santa Claus really was.

One year I wanted a watch for Christmas. By this time mom and daddy had four other children, Barbara, Preston, Clarence and Anna. They did not have a lot of money, so my chance of getting a watch was very slim. When Christmas morning came, I did not get the watch. I was hurt, but I knew my parents had done the best they could for us. I got the usual clothes, candy, nuts, fruit, and cookies. We had turkey for dinner, and plenty of good food. I played with my little brothers and sisters toys for a while, and then I decided to go over to Aunt Evelyn's to see what Sophie and Harold got for Christmas.

We lived on St. Luke's road then. As I walked from our yard toward the road, I noticed something on the ground, glittering in the sun. I could not believe my eyes. I stooped down and picked it up. It was a brand new ladies Benrus watch. I knew that only God could have put that watch there. It was my Christmas present from Him! I ran to Sophie's house, yelling, "I got a watch, I got a watch for Christmas!" I did not know anything much about prayer, but I knew that He had given me the desire of my heart. I recognized divine goodness and greatness at an early age.

~*Golden Rule and School Days*~

CHAPTER 5

I attended the elementary school for coloreds on Morris Street in Fruitland. This school was an extension of the first colored school which was located on Division Street, near Slab Bridge Road about 1907. Between 1910 and 1912 the county built another school on Morris Street and did away with the one on Slab Bridge Road. The building was a simple, three room structure with outdoor toilets. This was the school I entered as a first grader in 1939.

We had to walk about four miles to and from school; rain, shine, snow or blow. We stayed home a lot during the winter unless we got a ride. We were allowed to warm up before class started. Some days my hands were so cold that I had to put them in cold water before going to the stove. I welcomed the nice warm spring days; however, I was late many mornings. I spent a lot of time picking wild flowers for my teacher and buying candy and bubble gum at the store. I enjoyed the walks winter and spring.

The school day started at 9:00 AM. We had to line up on the outside, sing a song, salute the flag, and then march single file to our respective classrooms. The patrols helped to keep us in order. Those who misbehaved were paddled by the principal. The first and second graders were exceptions. They were disciplined by their teacher. We studied from 9:00 AM to 10:30 AM, had recess for 30 minutes, lunch at 12:00 noon to 1:00 PM, another recess at 2:00 PM, and then were dismissed at 3:30 PM.

The teachers were Mrs. Garrison (grades one

and two), Mrs. Frances (grades three and four); Mr. Handy (grades five to seven), later Mr. Brooks. They were very interested in the students and we knew it. We were encouraged to make something of ourselves. Mr. Brooks was the principal. At times he had to leave school to attend, special meetings in Salisbury. I was selected to be in charge of our room while he was gone. I was a seventh grader. This made me feel important and gave me a great desire to be a school teacher. I had to write down the names of problem students and report to him when he got back. A few of the boys threatened me and dared me to write their names on my list. One of them was Leighhunt Conway. We lived in the same neighborhood, so naturally he would start a fight after school. I had a lot of battles with him and I reported him each time, even if I did beat him. Mr. Brooks would whip him when he got to school the next day. He finally got the message that I would report him.

At times we had a few fights with white children who called us "niggers" as we passed by their school. The teachers had to come out to stop us from throwing stones at each other and name calling. In time, we learned to tolerate them and they decided to leave us alone.

I also got insults from some of the kids at our school. They called us poor because we lived on the farm. I had never thought of being poor until they made fun of my clothes and talked about the house we lived in. We lived in an old farm house, with outdoor toilets and no electricity. They made me ashamed of our house. I became extremely bitter and ended up in many more fights. I was determined that someday I would show those mean children that we were not poor.

I went home from school frustrated almost every day I tried to find a way for revenge, but instead, the Lord led me to read the 23rd Psalm.

> *"The Lord is my Shepherd, I shall not want. He maketh me to lie down in green pastures ....Thou   preparest a table before me in the presence of mine enemies."*
> *(Psalm 23:1, 2, 5)*

Even then, as a child, God had come to my rescue. I found peace and contentment as I read that Psalm, and fell asleep many nights with my little pocket New Testament in my hand.

No matter what happened I was always ready for school the next day. I had a few close friends at school, besides Sophie, they were Virginia Waters, a neighbor, Mayola Harmon, Sarah Deal, Mary Hester and Martha Townsend. I went home with Mayola often, since she lived near the school. I was especially drawn to her grandmother because she talked to us about Jesus, and being good, and doing things that were right. We remained friends throughout my elementary school days.

This was during the Depression. Things got so bad that school children in our area were given hot lunches, which consisted mainly of beans (navy or large lima's), prunes, homemade biscuits and butter. At lunch time, we were lined up, and fed one room at a time; usually the first and second graders were served first, then the older children.

Some of the sixth and seventh grade girls helped to wash the dishes and clean up after lunch. I don't remember how long this lasted, but the food was very good.

Some phenomenal experiences for me were times we talked with German prisoners. We had to pass by John H. Dulany's on the way to school. Cross and Bloekwell, a nationally known company, had large pickle vats (tanks) on the Dulany's property.

During World War II they used German prisoners as employees. This was exciting to me, because I had never seen or heard any one speak, who was not from our country or area. We talked with them almost every day. They taught us a few German words. Our main reason for talking with them was not to learn German, but to get one of those large pickles. They threw them over the fence to us. We made friends with our nation's enemies.

I loved school work, especially Geography, Social Studies, Music and Grammar. I didn't like

Arithmetic or Science. It was the stories about children who lived in foreign lands that fascinated me. I wondered what kind of food they ate and what kinds of clothes they wore. I related to the children in each country we studied. The mountain and Arctic regions astounded me. I could not understand how the people could live in regions like Alaska and Scandinavian countries. I studied the encyclopedia at school and read as much as I could about people of the world.

I also enjoyed reciting poetry. I memorized a poem by Henry Wadsworth Longfellow, entitled, *The Village Black Smith*, when I was in the seventh grade. I wrote many short poems and words to songs.

I had a special interest in the writings and lives of famous Negroes, especially Mary McCleod Bethune, James Weldon Johnson, Phyllis Wheatly, Booker T. Washington, and Paul Lawrence Dunbar. I was even more interested in the history and lives of Frederick Douglass and Harriet

Tubman because they were from Maryland, the Eastern Shore, and less than sixty miles from Fruitland. As I studied all of this, I always included the 23rd Psalm.

I graduated from the Fruitland School in May of 1946. On graduation night we did a program on the United Nations, which was organized in 1945. My assignment was the structure and responsibilities of the Security Council. I felt real important in my white dress explaining the functions of the Security Council to our parents, teachers and other guests. We made a few mistakes, but it was a very good presentation. Mr. Brooks was very proud of his seventh grade class. After graduation, the next step was high school. I was anxious to attend Salisbury High school. I had great expectations. I now knew that I wanted to be a school teacher.

~Too much Pride…
(My Teenage Years)~

CHAPTER 6

I entered Salisbury High on Lake Street in September of 1946. The high school kids from our area had to walk up to Fruitland to catch the bus to Salisbury. The bus came from Allen, a little community between Princess Anne and Fruitland. Mr. Naymon King owned and drove the bus. We had a real big thing going about Mr. Kings buses. They broke down quite often. We had to get off and walk to school. We were late almost every day. Many times we got to school just in time for lunch. What a thrill!

Salisbury High was so much larger than the

three room school I had gone to for seven years. I got lost the first day. There were two floors and a large auditorium, which was used for assemblies and physical education classes. Mr. Charles Chipman was our principal. I liked him because he was a strict disciplinarian. Problem students were whipped in his office. Mr. Chipman seemed to like me. He would see me walking down the hall with an apple and take it to tease me.

Most of my teachers were very dedicated to teaching and helping the students. Some of them were Miss Thelma (Rodgers Winder), Miss Flora Hariston, Mr. Charles Coates, Mr. William Hull, Miss Cleo Walston, Mrs. Jeanette Chipman, Miss Elaine Brown, Mr. William Owens and Mr. Franklin Waller. Mr. Waller taught U.S. History, my favorite subject. He saw my interest in history and encouraged me to go to college to study it.

My high school days were exciting. I met new friends from other parts of the county. They were Nina Taylor from Head of The Creek-Quantico,

Joan Wright from Wetipquin, Regina Barkley from Allen, Marian Gordy from Delmar, Isabella Nutter from Nanticoke, Ruth Nutter from Salisbury, Barbara Conway from White Haven. I had never heard of some of those places even though they were in Wicomico County. I admired the upper classman, especially the seniors. They always looked so distinguished standing on the halls, monitoring us little freshman. I could not wait until I became a senior.

On Saturdays a few of my friends, including Nina Taylor and Barbara Ann Brooks from Fruitland, and I attended the football games at Maryland State College in Princess Anne. Nina had a special reason for going – a young man who later became her husband. Barbara Ann and I had several reasons for going, such as handsome football players, and college boys in general. Our favorite player was Sylvester "Swifty" Polk, though no relation to me. He was an all American, very popular on the campus and entire East Coast. The college girls beat us to him, but we had a lot of fun. We pushed our way through the crowd to congratulate him after the games. He called me his "little" sister.

Ruth and Isabella Nutter, not related, were part of my study team. We studied together often. Isabella was proficient in English, Ruth was excellent in all the subjects; especially math and science, and I was good in history, so we had a real good group. I was attracted to Ruth because she professed to be a person with strong spiritual roots. Her grandmother belonged to the same church affiliation as my grandmother. I did not belong to any church, but when we filled out applications, I put my home church as St. Mary's Baptist Church. I enjoyed listening to Isabella talk. She was born and raised up in Boston, Massachusetts. I particularly liked to hear her say "Boston."

About ninety percent of the students in my class section from grades 8-11 went on to college and became professionals, most of them in the teaching field. By the time I reached the eleventh grade my mind was made up to be a history teacher. This meant a lot of hard work and saving money for school.

I worked in the fields and at other odd jobs during the summer to save money for clothes. The children had made fun of my clothes back in elementary school, so now I would show them who had the best clothes. I brought skirts and sweaters to match, several pairs of shoes (black and white saddle oxfords were the "in" thing then). I bought a new winter coat every year. I was always fortunate and blessed to find good paying jobs. For about three summers I lied by putting my age up to work at Campbell Soup Company, operating a canning machine. That job paid almost $100 a week and double time on Sundays. That was a lot of money then! I had a real ball working there because they also hired college boys from such schools as Hampton Institute, North Carolina A&T, Savannah State, Virginia State College and many others. I opened a bank account and things were looking up for me. I was finally coming out on top, so I thought. This did not last long before my head started swelling with pride. I bought clothes just to look good and tried to out dress the other girls at school. Seems like the moment you start acting prideful, everything goes wrong! Everyone always seemed to admire my beauty, along with being "light skinned" with long hair.

This attitude soon led to much rebellion and trouble. My parents were very strict, so I began to "*steal out*" with my friends. My school work started to decline and my grades got extremely poor. I hid my report cards, or made some kind of excuse, such as owing library fines, so my parents would not find out. They never went to parent teachers meetings, so I got by with it. I found myself struggling with the whole idea of staying in school. I stopped going to church with my grand-mother, but I knew I was wrong and struggled with the negative influences that were trying to get my attention. I had dreams about going to Sunday-School and church. I finally attended a local Methodist Church about two Sundays out of the month. I went there because they did not require as much of me as my grandmother's church. I could wear make-up and dress the way I wanted to. I did not join that church but instead, I decided to join our softball team and played softball almost every Sunday during the summer.

At the age of sixteen, I saw in a vision that I would be used in some type of ministry. If I did not accept the call, I would loose of control of my life. This caused much concern in my spirit for a while, but not enough to change my plans. My brother Billy, became a minister and started preaching while he was in high school. I knew he was praying for our family, and me in particular. I distinctly remember coming in late at night, after twelve o'clock, and finding Billy sitting up reading the bible. Something told me it did not take all of that. I thought we were both too young to be stuck in church. After all, there were so many things that I could do. I could go to college and be a teacher, or travel and see the world. I did not think this could be accomplished if I hung around Fruitland.

I also knew, inside, that I could become a famous singer if I really wanted to because I could sing pretty good and had the looks to go along with the voice. Thoughts of fame started to saturate my thinking. I had to do something big… this little life was becoming way too small for me! It sounded good to my proud ego………funny thing is that no matter how proud I felt, I still felt unworthy……… not good enough. So I started going to the local clubs and beer taverns to sing where the people encouraged me.

The neighborhood we lived in was called "Moonshine." The name came from the kind of business that had gone on in that area for years, bootlegging (selling homemade whiskey). Moonshine had a total of ten houses, three beer taverns, and a baseball field. The usual crowds at those taverns were farmers, field hands, and factory workers. Most of them were from Dulany's Canning Factory and mill workers, who came there from Friday night to Sunday to unwind from a hard weeks work. Since I was too young to drink, we as young people played the juke boxes and slot machines, danced and mixed in with the crowd. I hit the jackpot often. Each time, I felt condemned when I got home with a pocket full of nickels. I did not listen to my heart when it kept telling me what I was doing was wrong.

I went on in my own way. Defiance continued to dominate my life. I kept feeling that I had to prove myself, to whom exactly I'm not totally sure, but many emotions and the need to be needed affected my soul. I was doing ok because I was getting on track, regardless.

There was a young man from one of our nearby towns who was interested in me. I had, once before, let him know that I was not interested in a relationship because I needed to focus on my goals. Eventually I did agree to go on a date with him and discovered that he was a decent young man. Feeling, once again, that I could handle things, one thing led to another and I found myself, pregnant at the age of sixteen going on seventeen. No one is perfect, and that's a fact. The young man was a nice fellow, but I was not ready for marriage. That's what he wanted, and I had no intentions of settling down. He went in the Army, and I dropped out of school in the twelfth grade. We never saw much of each other after that point. This was the most devastating, degrading thing that could ever happen to my pride, making me ashamed to go back to school the next year. This should have been enough to cause me to accept the fact that I needed to change, but it was not. There I was a teenager about to become a mother. I did not know any-thing about being a mother. How could I take care of the baby? I went through months of crying and feeling sorry for myself. I remember begging God to let me go back to school during one of my moments of agony. Then I began to think that I could still become something great, and be recognized in the community. The feeling of rejection, and the desire for recognition led me to a quest for acceptance.

Meanwhile. . . . Down in the big city of New

Orleans, Antoine "Fats Domino," had just recently been re-signed to his record label "Imperial Records." His famous piano style and singing was becoming a resounding staple all along the Gulf Coast, and headed up to the east coast. His music was rising on the charts, particularly his song called, *"Rockin' Chair."* He was being called the "Blues King" because his piano playing style was phenomenal, and he was still growing. Fat's brother-in-law, Harrison Verrett, was one of the greatest influences on him as a young boy. He taught him how to play piano chords and would write the notes on the keys to make it much easier for Fats to learn. So, along with his natural talent, becoming as great as he was in his gift was inevitable. His family was growing there in New Orleans and life was becoming *"Grand, Very Grand."* He was round about 24 years old now. Many white DJ's were giving high praises to Fats and his unique talent. During the same year, another one of his songs called *"Goin' Home"* became a number one hit. Concerts and local shows for his band were coming like wild fire…work was constant and his family time at home was slowly, changing. Fats loved clothes, shoes, booze and women; but then again, what man would turn down such temptation?

This life style was really becoming not so bad for a young man who stopped going to school at the age of fourteen to go to work to earn a living. A few of his concerts were blamed for causing the black and white audiences to "cross racial lines," or plain and simple, integration issues. His group, like many others at the time, performed in places where they could not even use the restrooms, not to mention eating in the same buildings as their white counter parts. This up and coming young musician, making up to $500 a night at the time, [which grew to be much larger], constantly away from home, being highly admonished, loved and cherished everywhere, with no one to answer to....

PART TWO

THE LONG JOURNEY

~My Quest For
Acceptance~

CHAPTER 7

The word acceptance means a favorable reception or approval. That was the most important desire of my heart at the time….to be accepted. I wanted to be a part of my community. Inside, I constantly felt like I was a nobody. Now that I had a child, I felt very insecure and self-conscious. I have since learned that the origin of insecurity is rejection. Why do so many of us fall into the trap of rejection? I felt like I was being observed without being accepted.

At that point, if just one person had told me that I could still accomplish something in life, then my story might have been different. But then again, this is how my journey was supposed to be and I've learned to embrace it! The desire to be loved and respected was a silent weapon that kept me in a web. I felt like I was always trying to untangle myself…I wanted to break away from the pattern of poverty and illegitimacy that had plagued our entire family for years. I was ashamed because I had to temporarily be a welfare recipient. I sought love in the wrong places, for all the wrong reasons. I needed something. I did not know then, that the only way to be accepted and to have the desires of my heart was for me to love me! The popularity and attention that I needed would have been different if I had known how valuable I was… But even at the ages of eighteen and nineteen, there's still so much to learn!

In an effort to find my place in the sun, I went to Brooklyn, New York in 1952 via Trailways bus. I left Julia, my two year old little girl, with my mother. My mother knew that I was hurting, but did not know how to help me. I decided that the big city was the place to go. I could get lost in the crowd. No one there would suspect that I had a child. I did not know anyone personally in New York, so I took a job working for a Jewish family.

God is so wise and merciful. He will allow us to make our own choices, and then waits patiently until we come to the realization that we can do nothing without Him. I made the choice. The job lasted about two months. I was hired to baby sit for $30.00 a week, Thursdays off, free food and a private room. By the end of the first month, I was a babysitter, cook, maid and housekeeper, with no days off and enough work for three people. Being a young single woman I was confronted with unwanted advances of certain gents in the area. Nothing too vulgar, but I just didn't need that in my life at that time. I was looking for *"ME"* and not another relationship! All this overwhelmed me so, that I lied and told my employer that my mother was sick and I had to go home. I quit and went to visit a friend of mine in Philadelphia.

My girlfriend was a clerk at City Hall in downtown Philadelphia. I was to stay at her mother's house until she could help me find a job. I tried to get a job where she worked, this did not work out because I couldn't type and was not qualified for any kind of skilled work. I filled out applications and rode the buses and subways from North Philly to South Philly almost daily. I learned a lot about the city as I looked for a job. My friend's mother was very nice to me. I ate with the family and had a nice place to sleep.

I found a job at a delicatessen, but soon learned that city life was not for me. My girlfriend went out to the bars and night clubs at eleven and twelve midnight. This was totally alien to my way of thinking. I was expected to keep up with the crowd. Where I came from, the back woods of Fruitland down on the farm, the people went to bed with the chickens! I tried to go along with the night crowd for a while, but decided that I had enough of Philadelphia and the big cities. I wanted to see my little girl and to take care of her. I quit the job and went back home to Fruitland. I had saved some money so I was not completely without cash.

Although I wasn't where I wanted to be in my life, I was feeling better because the passion that I had inside was re-ignited.

~*A Door Opens…..*~

Chapter 8

The old idea of being a singer sprang up again. I had kept in touch with some of the musicians in the area. They always let me know what was going on in town because I had been singing in a group, led by a guy named Donald Jones, prior to my pregnancy. Salisbury, Maryland was the hub of the lower eastern shore. It was the Mecca of up and coming "Stars." There was a nightclub in Salisbury called the "Blue Moon." Famous singers and bands usually came there from Philadelphia, Baltimore, Washington, D.C., and New York on weekends. The jazz band from Maryland State

College, now The University of Maryland Eastern Shore (UMES), which was only about fifteen miles from where we lived, also played at the Blue Moon frequently. My group sang there too.

I went almost every weekend to hear the groups and to learn something about singing. Since I had recently returned from my adventures of "Big City Life," my girlfriends, the few of us who hung out, were more than happy to resume our outings. You know how it is with your few best-friends. We spent time planning our outfits a week ahead of time. Most of us only had one phone per house, but you can rest assured that we had the lines all tied up with conversations about important topics like, hair, shoes, and clothes! During those days, there were no designer jeans. They were called dungarees or overalls which were mostly worn by men. The women wore the straight, pencil type skirts, and the A-line poodle dresses and skirts; button up blouses, some with ruffles, along with a little sweater or cardigan, and little pump shoes, … *they were my favorite…* although we loved the oxfords too. Penny loafers were very popular too. Girdles were a big seller too because we had to keeps those hips tamed. We had fun swapping out different pieces of our clothes within our group of friends. We all loved smelling good too. We wore deep red and pink lipsticks on special occasions, but we enjoyed the pastels colors too. We had nice, wool, topper jackets with *"handmuffs"* and scarves in the winter.

Of course, we would invade our mom's jewelry drawers. Pierced earrings were barely heard of back then so clip on earrings and broaches were all the rage. My friends, who needed to, would have their hair pressed and curled to a "T." Most of the time I would use water and a hair pomade, called "Dixie Peach." I had, what was known as "good hair," *(although, I say no matter what type of hair you have, your hair is good to you)*.

Since we were some of the best dressed young ladies that would go up to Salisbury on the weekends from the country, Fruitland, naturally we had to keep up our best dressed reputation. Planning how we would get into the city and how we would get back was important. We didn't have our own cars but at times we would occasionally get rides. We would never ask our parents to drop us off at the club, even if they had a car. So most of the time we succumbed to the local cab company for 25¢ to 50¢ per ride, even though there were times when 25¢ was hard to come by. I didn't know it then but this night at the "Blue Moon" would be special. I had no idea how this night would change my whole life......*MY-WHOLE-LIFE*.........

It was February, of 1954... Saturday night. We got out of the cab and headed towards the entrance of the club. There was a set of long, thin, stairs to climb with a small platform at the top of the stairs. The bathroom was on the right, not very big, and the door to get into the venue was on the left. Admission was generally about 50¢ to $1, sometimes free, depending on what was going on that night. I remember that it was a cold but clear evening. I remember so well as I gazed up at the sky, it was dark yet the moonbeams were bright and crisp, almost telling their own story, just delightful. On this particular night, the guest star was a very popular rock and roll recording artist. It was Fats Domino, and he had come to Salisbury Maryland! He had just made a new record that was gaining top ratings in the Billboard magazine and throughout the nation. I enjoyed listening to him play the piano and singing on the radio. When my friends and I went into the show that night, we sat at a table very close to the bandstand. We were so glad that we had called the cab early because the club was overly crowded that particular night because of the anticipation of the guest star's appearance. We were so excited. The music started and the crowd went wild. Some were dancing the bop and some were watching the star and his band playing their instruments. It was something else.

While sitting there listening to the group perform I began to dream a thought of me as their female vocalist. My imagination was dreamy, I was no longer in the club. I was behind the microphone, I was Diana Ross, Nancy Wilson and Gladys Knight combined…As I came back to reality, I quickly spontaneously began to clap along with rest of the crowd as the tune was ending… still, somehow, imagining how much fun it would be traveling and meeting people across the country, ….and the music played on.   The scent of perfume and cigarette smoke began to fill the place. Beer, house liquors, and moonshine were the club staples. The smell of food from the "The Postal Card" restaurant   near the club, set a deliciously aromatic tone, making all who indulged in the adult beverages hungry.

Young and old, men and women who flocked to the club, of course were dressed to the nines. These places were known as a part of the *"Chit'lin Circuit,"* little back street clubs that were known for their Rockin'-n-Rollin' sounds of fabulous, mostly black entertainers. Many well-known artists such as Ray Charles, Lloyd Price, and James

Brown did regular appearances on the *"Chit'lin Circuit."*

We were just having a good time when one of my girlfriends leaned towards me and told me she noticed the rock and roll singer had been gazing in my direction as if he were under a spell during the whole show. My cousin Sophie said, "Chile', he could not keep his eyes off of you!" I shrugged off the comment and said to myself 'yeah right, all these cute girls in here and he's lookin' at me?' Shortly after that I was proven to be wrong. To my surprise, as it turned out, the singer had inquired about my identity. The club owner, Slim Marshall, came to our table during intermission and told me that someone wanted to meet me. I knew Slim as a really nice man, so I said, "OK." As I carefully walked beside the owner towards the side of the band area, I nervously straightened myself up. My mind was in awe as wondered who this person was. I wondered if Sophie was right…and…. she was! The person turned out to be the leader of the band, Fats Domino, "Antoine Fats Domino," one of the most famous and successful recording stars of the 1950's. I could not believe this was happening to me. We were introduced and from that moment there was instant chemistry.

He was more than complimentary on my appearance. I could not help but notice his fancy clothes. He had on a light tan suit, with a light silk shirt with a bold printed red colored tie, with the most expensive looking shoes, I had ever seen. He wore the best jewelry that money could buy and he sure smelled good too. He had beautiful deep colored hair that was styled, in what had become, his signature waved hairstyle.

He asked me as many questions as he could, though I had to listen real good because of his resounding New Orleans slang like drawl.

He asked my age, if I was married or had a boyfriend, where I was from, and where I lived. By this time, he asked for my phone number so I gave it to him and he slipped it into his jacket pocket. Before we knew it, the intermission was over. I hurried back to my seat, with my heart pounding so fast, to enjoy the rest of the show. My girlfriends were questioning me to no end. "What did he say? What did he want? He likes you don't he? Ain't he married girl? He is cute though," and so on.

At the time I really didn't put that much thought beyond that meeting because I heard stories about those slick singers and how they met so many women while on the road traveling. Fats Domino asking for my phone number was not a big deal to me because I was not interested in becoming one of those young women. But for the moment, pure elation doesn't even begin to describe how I felt. He wanted to know *"ME"* and that was very flattering to a girl at my age. This man knew people all over the country and wanted to know who *"I"* was.

The second half of the show was just as great as the first. As the show was coming to a close, the applause overshadowed everything. The crowd began leaving their seats heading for the band area and within seconds, there was no room to see anything. We knew the routine so my girlfriends and I headed for the exit to go down stairs to catch a cab and head home. We lived generally close together so we took the same cab and was dropped off according to where we lived. While we were in the cab we laughed and joked about the night's events and how much fun we had. We were getting louder by the minute. Every time the driver looked at us in his mirror we would get quiet, then start all over again with outburst of laughter.

When I got home I ran to the front door. As I put the key in I began to reflect back on things that he, "Fats," said to me about how I looked. I was immediately drawn back to the "Blue Moon," suddenly the reality of the night began to flow through my mind. I felt like I was 100 feet tall. Then it hit me .... something good had happened to me tonight. It was already late so I closed the door slowly behind me as I glided on air to my bed. I stopped at mom and daddy's door because my little girl, Julia was sleeping in their room. Slowly I opened the door and walked in to see my baby. She was in between mom and dad and looked so peaceful as I leaned in to kiss her goodnight. I loved my little girl and at times it seemed, she was all I had. As I begin to walk out of the room, mom said, "Ginny', that you"? I whispered "Yeah mom, thanks for watching the baby, go back to sleep." I gingerly closed the door to go to the other bedroom that I shared with my two younger sisters, Barbara and Anna Lee. They were sleep too, so I sat on the edge of our bed and began to change my clothes. I kicked my shoes off before I finished undressing, laid back on the bed for what was supposed to be a second, and there I went, off to dreamland, only to be awakened the next morning by my youngest sister Anna Lee, jumping on the bed.

~*Meeting Fats…..*~

CHAPTER 9

Mom always had something good cooking. Homemade flour biscuits were a regular part of Sunday breakfast and this particular morning was no different. Mom and dad always got up early to make coffee. While breakfast was being prepared my parents would talk over the day's events while enjoying the aroma of freshly brewed coffee. I got up to walk down the hallway to get my little girl from mom's room and was overwhelmed by the morning meal. What a good feeling.

Though last night was a magical evening I had not given much thought about it because of my reality. I had a child to care for and I loved my family. They helped me in any way that they could and being the oldest child, I was determined to do something great regardless of the choices I had made up to that point in my life.

After a little while we all ate breakfast and helped clean up the kitchen. Everybody had chores, even my younger brothers. We had a small black and white television with a couple of limited channels and after house work was done, my younger brothers and sisters, were allowed to watch for a little while. It had gotten to be about noon time and I had gone back into the room with my little girl. In the midst of the sounds of my brothers and sisters chatter, there came a rather loud knock at the door. Mom answered the door and we could hear the sound of a man's voice. As he was speaking, we all began to walk towards the front of the house to see who it was. Staying in the back ground, I heard his permeating voice say, *"Hello Ma'am. My name is Bernard. How do you do?"* Mom suspiciously replied, *"Pretty good."*

He continued, *"Ma'am my boss sent me down here to ask your permission, to bring your daughter "Virginia," to Salisbury cause he just wants to talk to her."* Mom responded, *"How you know where she lived and who's your boss?"* He replied, *"I'm sorry, 'Ma'am, my boss is Fats Domino, the rock n roll singer. I'm his chauffeur, I drives all over the country fo him, and he met your daughter up at the Blue Moon Club last night. The owner Slim, giv'em de address and he, my boss, give it ta me and told me to find her, Virginia."* Mom says, *"Oh, I know Slim, but where you want to take my daughter?"* He says, *"Like I said Ma'am, I just needs to take her to the club so's he can talk to her and I promises to bring her back, safe, soons dey finish talkin'."* Mom says hesitantly, *"Well,...I don't know."* He asked again, *"Ma'am Please, I promise I'll take care of her and bring her back safe, cause my boss told me if I don't bring her back, "He Go'ne Fire me! Please Ma'am I promise! I needs dis job."* Mom says, *"Well, you promise?"* Bernard replied, *"Yes Ma'am."* So mom responded *"Alright then, but you know you got to bring her right back, cause I know Slim good...you know what I mean...?"* Then with a half-smile of relief he said *"Thank you Ma'am, I promise."* Just then, daddy walks up from the barn and said, *"let her go sister,"* that's what he called mom, "sister." *"If Slim giv'em the address, he must be alright."*

I walked back to the room to grab a jacket. My sister was holding my daughter. I kissed them both and then off I went in a big, black, long, shiny limousine. I glanced out the window and smiled, while laughing inside, as I saw my whole family, protectively gathered and gazing out of the window as we left. As a young lady, not only was I stunned, I was in total shock because it was so unbelievably dreamlike. I had hardly ever seen a limousine, let alone someone sending one for me as a ride. The fact that he went out of his way to find me way down in the country was enough to realize he was interested in me.

The limo ride to Salisbury was the longest ride ever. My curiosity and nervousness began to get the best of me. I was riding in a car with a man I had never met before. Suppose he didn't do what he said. Suppose he was not who he said he was. The driver, Bernard, began a light hearted conversation with some small talk. I soon realized that this was just as awkward for him because, after all, he was the one with his job on the line.

Finally, we reached our destination. Bernard parked the limo and promptly and properly, came around to open my door. As I got out of the car, I saw Slim's smiling face, and instantly the anxiety was somewhat relieved. I still did not know why this man wanted to talk to me or why he sent the driver to get me. I knew he had expressed an interest the night before, but to this extent? Or maybe it was my big break for singing that I daydreamed about. The suspense was almost unbearable but I remained as calm as I could on the outside. Inside, I was a nervous wreck.

Slim was standing in the door way and greeted me with a bigger smile as he signaled with a head movement that someone was waiting inside. The club was not open yet but Slim had opened it up for Fats to close last minute details for Saturday night's show. As I went in, I could see Fats look up to make eye contact with me as a genuine gracious smile took over his whole being. It was probably a smile of relief because he was not for certain that I would meet with him. He got up and walked to greet me. As he got closer, he reached out to shake my hand and nervously, yet obviously excited, thanked me for coming. He actually said that he didn't think I was coming for sure.

He led me to some seats towards the back where we ended up talking for more than 2 hours. As promised, he made sure I returned home safely afterward. When I came into the house mom wanted to know everything, of course. I let her know as much as I had found out from Fats and like me, she could not believe it. She was cautiously, more excited than I was! Daddy was just daddy, listening but saying nothing. I guess he figured that I was grown.

I really didn't know what would come of this meeting because Fats had a wife and family in New Orleans, where he lived, and I had already heard about his situation. I was not planning on becoming the other woman because that's one line that I never wanted to cross.

By this time my parents had been married for a while. They had ups and downs, just like all marriages, so even though I was single, I totally respected the institution of marriage and family. During our conversation I informed Fats of my respect for marriage and he seemed to understand. I was so interested in advancing my singing career that I was willing to spend the kind of time it would take to learn all I needed to know.

Fats had assured me and re-assured me, that he was going to stay in touch…and he did. He began to call me daily from everywhere the band was performing. Fats even asked about the possibility of me coming on the road with him. He said not only would he take care of my little girl's needs, but my parents as well while I traveled. Since mom was home, and my daughter was not old enough for school, I made arrangements with her to care for my Julia. Within weeks, he sent for me, thus a relationship of some sort, had begun to bloom. I say of some sort because it was, in the beginning, a close friendship and I still wanted to develop my singing.

I, as a young lady from the country around pigs, chickens, and cows, had *NEVER* been around so much excitement in my life! When I first took a real look at New York City from the other side of the tracks, I was quietly at a loss for words. Overwhelmed was not the word. I was being waited on hand and foot. I felt like a princess, that's how Fats treated me, and no less than. I was highly impressed. It was first class all the way. A young lady's dream.

Even with all the fame, black people still had to

use separate restrooms and certain eating areas. At first I felt a little insecure because this was all new to me. However, Fats let all the band members know that I was to be cared for. Whatever the "Boss" said was bond. Eventually I grew to be a special part of the "on the road family" and had a great friendship with most of the band members.

Fats and I were becoming inseparable. The passion was unbelievable. The times that he wanted me to be on the road with him grew from days, to weeks from weeks, to months. Instead of learning how to be a singer, I found myself involved in an affair that lasted for many years. Fats was married, but I was blinded to the consequences at that point. I had no desire to be involved in this adulterous relationship, but I just could not bring myself to leave it. At first, I thought it was the fame and money, but I was just blinded by the love of it all.

During those years, I traveled across the USA with Fats and his top rated band. There was a lot of mistrust at times when it came to the band getting paid. Cash was the main means of pay and certain ones collecting at the door could not be trusted and would often skim their personal cut off the top. It started happening so much that Fats began to have the money sent up to me in the hotel room. I was very good in handling the money and keeping it organized as well. At the end of the night members in the band would come up to the room to get their pay through me. I would already have the money neatly sorted out and stacked under the mattress ready to be distributed. I handled it like a business woman and this made the guys happy. Real trust was constantly being established. Fats would send his personal chauffeur all the way from Philadelphia to Maryland, just to pick me up to do the job and be with him.

After being on the road with Fats, I had thoughts of all those people who had called me poor. So when his Chauffeur drove up to my house in a big pink, Eldorado Cadillac, in my mind I said, "Look at me now." I thought this would compensate for the shame of being a poor little rejected, insecure, country girl.

We played in some of the largest night clubs, theaters, and auditoriums in the country, such as the Apollo Theater in NYC; we stayed in the Waldorf Astoria, Hiltons and Sheratons nationwide. Those hotels were just outstanding. We had so much fun together. Fats and I were becoming a team. This did not erase my background, but made matters even worse. My friend, Fats, was very sensitive and extremely jealous. He questioned everything that I would do. When I was not with the group, every minute had to be accounted for. I had to give details of my daily errands. I could not leave home for any length of time without giving a full explanation of where I had been and how long I had been out of the house. I stayed close to the telephone, so that I would not miss any calls. Even if it took a little time for me to get to the phone, he would get suspicious. No matter where the group was, I had to be prepared to leave home at any time to travel to wherever they were playing in the states. This was really becoming the beginning of something I had never experienced before. I was a strong headed woman, but when you are being taken care of completely your thinking starts to change. I was beginning to realize the price this lifestyle was costing me, yet, what else was I doing with my life at this point? It was love and pain at the same time.

The bondage was even more severe when I had my first child by him in 1955, Ronnie. He was beautiful. He had a head full of large beautiful curls, more of my complexion, just under 8 lbs., born in Maryland. At the same time, back at home in New Orleans, a few of his other children were being born or had been born within some of the years we were seeing each other. Even in between shows there were still other women willing to comply, at any cost. I was no fool. He was still a man, who was a star.

Although the handwriting was slowly being written on the wall, our story together was still a blue print. I knew that this affair was wrong and thought that I could quit whenever I wanted to. The longer I put it off, the deeper the involvement. The deeper the involvement, the more rewards and enticements. Every time I felt the guilt about my new life with him, he made me feel that it was alright and there was nothing wrong with our involvement. I would forget about how I was feeling, and the cycle would start all over again. In so many ways it was a fabulous life. I can't really explain why, except something inside made me feel proud to be the "mistress" of this famous singer. Maybe it was because I was so poor as a child that I became very comfortable in this position. I was very wealthy in many ways because he made sure that I had *everything* that I needed, as well as all the money I wanted. He was fast becoming a multi-millionaire, especially during those years. Fats promised to totally take care of his children that I had borne, and he kept his word. I thought, I was happy…

I remember walking down the street in our

neighborhood, hearing someone say, "Oh, there goes Fats Domino's girlfriend, she lives right here" I was living in Salisbury then. By now I had Karen, my beautiful caramel baby girl, with a mix of curly and straight hair. She was just under 8lbs with combination features of Fats and myself. Now I had a boy and girl by this man. My home became a constant view for the curious. People came by my house to see the children. My children were celebrities, and they were gorgeous, so I dressed them accordingly. I bought their clothes from the biggest most expensive department stores all over the world. Most regular women could only dream about this lifestyle and price…was no object. When I wasn't able to travel, Fats would have things sent to the house for the children and myself. By now my Mom and Dad, along with a few of my siblings, would help watch the children while I was traveling around the country. My oldest daughter, Julia, was becoming old enough to help too. I went to New York and Philadelphia to shop. Friends told me that I would be crazy to give up all of this popularity, money, and clothes now that I was looked up to. I constantly remembered how children had made fun of my clothes and made fun of our house when I was young. Now "I" had my own house; purchased by the help of Fats; a big beautiful brown house with beautiful trees and property, in an all-white neighborhood, they called California because only white people could afford to stay there. What more did I need? I was having a ball living like some young girls could only dream of. Life was wonderful, but there was something terribly wrong inside of me. Everything comes at a cost, sooner or later. I had it all beauty, fame, and fortune. I thought it would make me happy.

In time, I became miserable in my condition. Occasionally, I would feel guilty because I knew what I was doing was not right, but the thoughts would always fade away. I had three children out of wedlock with no prospects of marriage, unless he got a divorce. Deep down inside I did not want to go through this. I shrugged off the idea every time he brought it up. He constantly let me know that he was ready to end his marriage, if only I would agree to become his wife. I was so tormented. It seemed like every week divorce was his main subject. This was so unpleasant for me because it required me to make a definite choice. Even though we were deeply involved, I just couldn't bring myself to cause even more pain to his family. I had come to know so much about them through him. He had actually let his wife know that he was going to be leaving her for a woman in Maryland... me. He wanted to marry me. She did leave him for a short period of time but soon returned. I had so many thoughts, positive and negative. I felt like I was going to lose my mind. The pressure was unbelievable. After all, there was still a chance that he would do to me what he was doing to his family at home. Even though we were an item, I had been hearing rumors of other women as well as possible other children. There were even other issues involved, however, I was a large part of the puzzle. The question of him wanting to marry me, never stopped. Somewhere in the back of my mind, I had learned that this was not God's plan for the family, yet I could not make up my mind to quit. I had lost my desire to travel with Fats, but I went anyway. This lifestyle was so addictive. But our relationship had become an unusual tumultuous one, spiritually, physically and emotionally. The bickering, possessiveness, and out of control, "control" was quite bizarre, to me, since he was a married man. This was a predicament that only a miracle could change.

Nothing but the grace of God kept me from being an alcoholic or becoming a drug addict. I was so strong, yet so weak. Drugs and alcohol were always available in this type of circle. Most of the young men in the group were heavy drinkers. Some had very serious drug problems. In fact one young man who was about 27 years old died from an overdose while we were on the road. They called him *Papoose*. I stayed in the hotel room most of the time, while the group performed in the nightclubs and hotel ballrooms. A midst all of the bright lights, fine clothes and other extravagances, there was something about that life style that did not agree with what was going on inside me. There was still a vacuum that had not been filled.

The turning point came one night in Philadelphia. The group stayed out almost all night. This gave me time to cry out to God. I promised Him that night, that if He allowed me to get back home, I would not go back on the road again. I went home the next day and stayed about two months, then the call came and I went back. I was trapped, locked into this situation and unable to do anything about it. Fear gripped my heart each time I thought about quitting. One of my biggest fears was being on my own with very little education, with children, a home to care for, and no job. As soon as I got back home, I could feel something inside, reminding me of the promise I had made earlier. The thought of lying to the Almighty made me a miserable creature. I had now reached the zenith of my horrible state.

Once again I found out I was pregnant. My handsome little boy Anton, my fourth child, was born in June early 1960's, he too had smooth beautiful brown skin, curly hair, 7 lbs. with even more stronger features of Fats. I began to seriously look for a way out. I remembered some of the messages from my grandmother's pastor. I believed that God would help me if I got serious enough. My quest had led me to a tunnel, where I hoped to see the light at the end of it... This would be the beginning of the end.

~*Light At The End of The Tunnel*~

CHAPTER 10

A few days after I was back home, a bible salesman came to my house. With only a small amount of money I bought a big family bible by paying a partial payment and the balance spilt up to pay over some months, *something like lay-away,* and began to read. When we are serious I believe help comes right on time. The bible salesman came when I desperately needed to communicate with God. I knew very little about the scriptures, but I remembered reciting the twenty-third psalm when I was in elementary school. I heard many sermons at my grandmothers' church, but could only think of the ones about going to hell.

I read the twenty-third Psalm every night after the children were sleep. I had begun to even remember several scriptures from my childhood. I soon understood that the way I was living was most definitely wrong. I saw fornication, adultery, and especially the illegitimacy that I was involved in for what they were; unacceptable anymore, in my life. So many times the culprit is, self. We tend to seek to please ourselves no matter what the ultimate consequences.

Each time I committed, what I felt to be wrong to me, I could feel the struggle deep down inside and I knew that it was such strong a tug of war for my very soul. I wanted so deeply to do the right thing but there was no way I could do it on my own, no way.

When I read Revelations 3:20-21, I really wanted to be an over comer. I kept reading these scriptures until finally, one night in desperation, I cried out to God, again. I promised, again, that if   He would get me out of the dilemma I was in, I would live for Him and do whatever He wanted me to do.

The wooing of divine love was so strong, that of my own free will, I fell into the arms of redeeming grace. I, at that time, submitted my life to God. I realized that I had been running from reality as fast as I could. I remembered what my grandmother's pastor had told my brother and me years ago, "You two children are marked out for God's work, and He has a work for you to do." I did not know what all that meant then, but now it was coming clearer to me that I was to be a leader not a follower.

The reading and praying continued for about a year before I got bold enough to go to a local church. The light was beginning to shine and I could see a little beam ahead of me. The church that I went to was an old-time Pentecostal Church of God In Christ. They had a testimony service. This is where the people stand and tell what God has done for them. As I sat there in the back of the church, a lady stood and began to tell how God had helped her in a certain situation. She said that she prayed and he delivered her from deep sin. She expressed how clean and refreshed she felt. It seemed as if she was giving my life story at that time. I was asking Him to do for me what He had done for her. I did not go up when altar call was made, but as I left that church, I *believed* that God could do the same thing for me. I wanted what she had. Number one being, peace of mind.

I continued to read the psalms when I got home that Sunday night. I prayed and asked God to help me as He had helped the woman in the church. I thought of how Mom Sally used to make us get down on our knees, so I got down on my knees and prayed. I prayed all night. The next morning I bathed, clothed and fed my children and sent them outside to play. I went back upstairs to my bedroom and resumed my praying and crying out. I asked Him to save me from my sins and set me free from this affair. About twelve o'clock, I became born again, in my bedroom. I heard the sweetest music that I had ever heard. It seemed like entire room lit up. It is still hard to express, but my room and body were illuminated with a beautiful light. I knew that God had changed me and something special was going on in my Spirit, Soul and Body. The room, house, yard outside, and everything looked new to me. It was as if scales had fallen from my eyes. I managed to tell my children that their mother was a new woman. I told them that I was going to live a different life from that day on. They were young, so they did not understand what was going on, but they knew that something strange was happening to me. This was in June of 1962.

I had a vision about three weeks after this experience. I had been fasting, praying, and reading the bible. A few hours after I had gone to bed one night, I was awakened by a very unusual sense of the presence in the room. I looked toward the window in the room and saw a white figure near the window. I did not hear anything, but it came close to the bed. I could not see His face; I knew it was Jesus, in the Spirit, standing with outstretched hands to me. I was so amazed that I could not say anything for a few minutes. When I could open my mouth, the only thing I could say was Jesus! Jesus! It then vanished, and I felt like I had been talking with Jesus. It was an experience that I shall never forget.

The next day I went to a local record shop and bought an album by Mahalia Jackson. The main song was *"I Found The Answer."* I played that song over and over again; sometimes all night. I particularly liked the very first verse because it described   exactly   where   I   was   inside   so poignantly. I had been so weak, so tired, as well as dismayed. I was under a great mountain of much despair. But even with all of this there was an undeniable light that shined so brightly upon my soul that made me free inside as I slowly began my climb to take my life back. It was my "new life!" Although it was just the beginning,   learning to pray answered so many questions and it was, and is the key.

With the exception of my mother, and brother Billy, the rest of my family didn't go to church or anything. They thought I was either mentally disturbed or deeply hurt. No one could even begin to understand the mental anguish, the hurt, the confusion, the torment or the psychological purging of a relationship like this unless you've been through it. It was like unto a type of death, except it never really goes away.

The one thing my family did know was that all of my conversation centered on Jesus Christ. I told everyone that I came in contact with that I had been saved and changed my entire life style. People began to notice that I looked different. One lady said I looked like a Nun. I suppose she meant I looked holy from the outside or my countenance was different.

My desire to go back on the road completely vanished. I called Fats and told him that God had set me free. I was now a Christian and would not see him again. I could feel the anxiety and fear begin deep down in my stomach. I had a strong idea of how he might react but still, I was not ready for it. I had made a firm decision in my life that made a new kind of sense to me. He was, shocked and extremely angry. He tried to convince me that I was confused or going off on the deep end. I had nothing against his belief, however, I knew I was changed. It was even more of a complete shock to him that I was no longer interested in our relationship. He was furious that I was through. He threatened to stop sending money for the children if I didn't come back on the road. He explained to me that he had a different type of future planned for us. This interaction went on for weeks. A few times that he called I knew he had been drinking, which made things worse. His forceful voice tones were greatly ignited. He did love me and I loved him. It was just that long term things did not look promising. There were far too many unfavorable statistics, and too many lives to hurt. He kept calling and calling but I refused to take his calls because the temptation of it all was still so very strong. It was overwhelmingly difficult to break away from that lifestyle. It had been years of everything being given to me. I just could not fall another time! I had to be free from this. It was the fight of my life and I was scared. Once again, I told him it was over, even if it meant that I had to get a job. I had not worked in years and the thought of it was horrific, but I believed God could and would care for us.

When you are involved with someone so popular, it may come down to your word against his. Would I appear to be just another groupie? When I knew that was so far from the truth? Because of his temper, in my mind I could hear a voice trying to frighten me by telling me, "The man will kill you if you don't go back!" Fats wanted to divorce his wife to marry me, but not many people knew this except some of his close friends like, Bernard his chauffer, who had become my confidant, Billy Diamond and Bill Boskent. The reality that I would not marry him after he had told his wife that he wanted a divorce was one of the main reasons for his anger. These were the secrets that had become such a great part of my life. This was extremely heavy territory to conquer in every way. However, I could not afford to live in the fear of what people might think any more. My decision had to be final this time, and at this point, nothing discouraged me; I was so happy in my soul that I refused to give in to those thoughts. The SON was shining in my heart and I could see and feel the light. Hallelujah! Now, I would have to depend totally on "HIM".

~*Walking By Faith,*
Not By Sight~

CHAPTER 11

"For we walk by faith, not by sight." (II Corinthians 5:7). I had four children, no job, a mortgaged house and no financial security. I had to learn to walk by faith. I could not see what was ahead. I had put away a little money, and after that was gone, my parents began to help with my family. I had not worked in years and I knew I had to get it together. With faith and fear at the same time, I went in to action. I had a dream, about a job at a store. It was a five and dime called McCrory's. The next day I went to that store and got a job in the hardware department. My *faith* was now at work. The Bible says, and I believe, we are destined to prosper and be in health even as our soul prospers. I worked in that store for two years until it burned. Then I found job at another five and dime, F.W. Woolworth's. The job at Woolworth's was very interesting. I was hired to replace the girl who worked in the pet shop and hardware sections. She stayed on the first two weeks to show me the routine. I had the pleasure of caring for guinea pigs, parakeets, canaries, iguanas, chameleons (lizards), white mice, hamsters, gold fish and tropical fish. My children were fascinated when they found out the kind of job I had. I learned fast and really enjoyed watching the expressions on the faces of little children as they came into the pet shop.

I also learned to use the cash register and became one of the main cashiers during the nine years that I worked there. I was able to use the job at Woolworth's to help with clothes, food and school supplies for my children. I charged items during the week and had it deducted from my pay check. Eventually, I started receiving child support from Fats via his lawyer, Charles Levy Jr. This went on for years until the kids got older and established personal relationships with their dad. A few times payments came directly from his wife in the form of money orders. I believe it took a "strong" woman to make those payments. I decided to join St. Mary's Baptist Church, near Princess Anne. My mother and most of our family were also members there. I studied the bible in a new way, each word seemed to stimulate my entire being. I got baptized that summer for the first time at Jason's Beach in Delaware. I came up out of the water shouting like the man in the Bible, who they laid at the gate called beautiful asking for alms. I too, went walking and leaping and praising God. This was a glorious time in my life.

After I joined the choir I traveled and I gave my testimony boldly. I no longer needed to be accepted or to have special attention. I joined the missionary society and was elected president. I spoke to women's groups, teenagers and unwed mothers.

Surely with all of this happening in my life, things were beginning to look up, right? I stayed in church six months, and then became involved with a local band leader. I took yet another detour. It happened so fast, that I did not realize what was going on. I took my eyes off my goals, only for a moment, but look what can happen in a moment. What was I looking for? Nevertheless, God is faithful. My friends began to pray for me and kept encouraging me to come back to church. After about three months I returned to church. Mercy and grace brought me back on the right road. I repented, and like the prodigal son, came back home to my Father, who was waiting with outstretched arms of love.

My desire to be a school teacher was rekindled. I began to believe that my faith would help me, if I applied myself. I was inspired to finish my education. This meant going back to school for my high school diploma. I studied hard.

Some friends helped with math and science. After a few tests, I received a Maryland High School Equivalence Certificate. Mr. Chipman, my former high school principal and an outstanding pillar of our community, wrote a letter of recommendation to the college. I was so happy. I had so many people who encouraged me during this time. There were a few that thought I was foolish to quit a full time job and go back to school. This did not deter me, I knew that I would make it through by faith. This was another "HUGE" step of faith.

I entered Maryland State College at Princess Anne, September of 1964. I was a student all over again, after being out of school for 14 years. As I walked on the campus, my mind went back to those football games that I had attended while in high school and how my heart had been set on going to Maryland State after graduation. Now, I had a chance to be a history teacher. I had been given yet another opportunity. This was a tremendous challenge. With the exception of Anton, my youngest child, everyone else in our house was in school. We had fun studying together. It was a real sacrifice because there were times when I could not be with the children and help them as much as I wanted to.

I had already jumped over one big hurdle since I had changed my life. Now another one had been set up for me. I was blessed so rapidly that somewhere between the excitement of entering college and endeavoring to succeed, I took another detour. I was doing well in the church and school. I just knew I could control my desires and resist temptation, after all, I had learned a lesson. I was sure the temptation would come, but surely I could handle them now. What I did not know was that something was determined in its effort to stop my success. I became involved again, with a college professor. I was four months pregnant by the end of my freshman year. I couldn't believe this was happening to me. I did not understand how or why, but something was drastically wrong in my life. I was supposed to be born again, a new woman. How could this happen again?

I finished the school year, and then tried to figure out how to solve my problem. The only solution was to get away from home and the area for a while. I was ashamed to face my children, my family, and my brothers and sisters at our church. My education was jeopardized and my testimony for Jesus Christ, I thought, was destroyed. I decided to go to New York with my brother Billy until the baby was born. He lived in Brooklyn.

My previous experience in Brooklyn should have been enough to deter another visit, but this one would only be for a short time. I knew that Billy loved me and would be a good person to talk with at this time. He had been preaching since he was a teenager and had counseled hundreds of people with many kinds of problems. I believed in his prayers. I called him and set the time of our departure. We were to leave during the month of August. I planned to take Ronnie and Anton with me and to leave Julia and Karen with my parents.

We left for New York the first Monday in

August via Trail ways bus. The boys were very happy. This was the greatest thing that could possibly happen for them. They had fun during the five hour trip from Salisbury to New York City. We arrived at the Port Authority bus station before dark. We had to wait about one hour for Billy to come over by subway to take us back to Brooklyn. The boys were still excited. I had felt like crying during the entire trip. When Billy arrived I had to go to the restroom to keep from bursting out in tears. I wanted to say to him, *"here I am your oldest sister and I've messed up again."* Billy was cheerful as usual. He inquired about the family back home and asked if we were hungry. I thank God for my brother. He knew how to deal with the problem. We bought some snacks, caught the subway and went home with him.

Billy had a wife and four children, so Ronnie and Anton were right at home when we got there. We were received with love and kindness. We stayed with them for about a month, and then I planned to move to a place of my own. The responsibility was far too much for Billy. He had done all he could. This meant searching for a room. I went out daily, up and down the streets of Brooklyn; I took Ronnie and Anton with me. We often stopped at a nearby park and zoo and watched the animals. I let the boys play for a while at the playground, and then it was back home after a full day of looking for a room.

I was feeling greatly inspired. One day as I was sitting on a bench in the park. The boys were playing; I was reading the bible and a major change happened in me at that time. I was pondering my situation and began to pray silently, asking God for the divine will for my life and for my children. I did not know what to say. I just looked up and said, "Here I am again. I need your direction now." I felt a pure love in a way that I had not experienced before. I sat there and cried tears of joy. Something inside of me seemed to open up. I was refreshed and renewed in the spirit of my mind. I wiped my eyes so that the boys couldn't see me crying. Then we started back to Billy's house.

We passed by a church as we left the park. I made up my mind that I would go to that church the next Sunday. It was only two blocks from where we were staying. The next Sunday morning I dressed the boys, put on the best dress that I had and went to that church. We had to wait until the doors were opened. We enjoyed the service. Ronnie said, "Mom that man can really preach!" Anton also enjoyed the children playing drums and singing.

Something tried to discourage me from attending church pregnant, but I was determined to go anyway. I had always sought to do my best, no matter how many times I failed. My destiny has been in the hands of a loving, forgiving God from the beginning. Guilt, tried to rule my thoughts, however, I only allowed peace. This came one night as I went to the altar. I cried out to God as David had done,

> *"Have mercy upon me, according to thy loving kindness, according to the multitude of thy tender mercies, blot out my trans-*

gressions. Wash me thoroughly from mine iniquity. For I acknowledge my transgressions. Create in me a clean heart, and renew a right spirit within me. "

He answered with tender mercy. The brothers and sisters prayed for my children and me. I put my family on their list and asked them to help us find a suitable place to stay.

Within a week, I ran into the home of a wonderful lady who rented rooms. It was a miracle because I was just walking along the street, about four blocks from my brother's home on Park place and saw the room for rent sign. I moved the first week in September. The room was on the third floor, on the quiet end of the hall where I could be to myself. The furniture was very simple, with a single bed, dresser, chest of drawer, a night stand and lamp beside the bed. The cost was $10.00 per week. I did not have a radio or television. This was the perfect place to think and pray about my life.

My mother came to visit us for a weekend. She took Anton and Ronnie back home with her.

She thought it would be better for me, especially after the baby came. I was left alone. The memory of how I felt in that room without my children brings tears to my eyes now as I write about it. Julia, Ronnie, Karen and Anton were all that I had. They were dear to my heart. I had started college so that I could get a decent job. I wanted to make enough money to buy nice clothes and things they needed. Things that I did not have as a child. I was so used to having anything that I wanted, with Fats. This was a hard pill to swallow but I had to bite the bullet to be free, for me. Every now and then, more often than not, the reminders of the life style and all of the material advantages that I had with Fats would often invade my thinking, second guessing myself and re-evaluating my final choices often. The temptation to return to that life was a recurring thought, even at this point in my life, especially when times were hard.

Although I had changed my life there were many hard and tempting lonely nights. I fought past the feelings of regret and self-loathing. My heart ached each time I walked by the park and watched the children playing. There was a catholic school a block away from my house. I could see the kids all dressed in their uniforms on the way to and from school. I often sat on the door step and talked to them as they passed by.

I thought of Julia, how quiet and sweet she was. She had always been very studious and obedient, except for the times she was with her best friend, Stephanie. They once tried to pull the wool over my eyes. They stayed out too late and Julia decided to sneak in through the living room window. Much to her surprise, I was standing there as she hopped in. Well, we settled the issue in a few moments. I had to laugh afterwards because it brought back memories of some of my foolish teenage pranks.

Julia was a great help with her brothers and sister. Ronnie was a typical youngster, full of mischief. He enjoyed games and sports, but most of all, television. Karen was a very outgoing child.

She had a mind of her own and spoke what she thought, regardless to how it sounded. But Ronnie led her around by the nose when they were younger, because she did whatever he did. They were my famous twosome. As they got older, Karen changed. I am reminded of how Ronnie and Karen had done exercises with me and one of them, Ronnie, because he was the oldest and the male, instinctively, always made sure that I had my chair ready before the show started. I can almost hear them say, "Mom, here's your chair."

Anton was very shy. Ronnie and Karen were my two little schemers, so he felt like he was left out of their plans. They treated him like the "little brother." Julia gave him a nick name, Boo. He always had a desire to help me. He once said, "Mom when I get big, I am going to buy you a new house and a new dress."

They all loved me. They enjoyed preparing breakfast in bed on my birthday. Since my birthday was on the 4th of July we had a grand celebration. They had more fun than I did. I asked God to help me make it up to them. I wanted to be a good mother more than anything else at the time.

I did the only thing that I knew to do, pray and read the bible. I prayed many nights all night on my knees beside the bed. I went to a Baptist church around the corner from where I lived. The pastor and members encouraged me to fellowship with them. The pastor was Rev. Cooper and I was constantly encouraged. I remember his words to me, "You don't have to continue down the same road. God wants to use you in the ministry." They also persuaded me not to stay in the room alone too much and promised to help when the baby came. I stayed in that room for two months, went to church at least twice a week and visited my brother and his family. I prayed through and I got the answer. It was to leave New York after the baby was born. I was to go back home and finish college.

I had the assurance that "this time," *"this time,"* I was on the right road. I had taken my last detour. I was determined that this was the last child out of wedlock. I would not have any more children, not because of the use of birth-control pills or some other device, but because I would not have sex again until I had the right husband. I believed that all things are possible. I knew deep down within my inner man that I could win over this flesh with God as my help. I now had the power to excel, and not in my own strength. The pastor at that Baptist church had told me that I did not have to let the choices I had made ruin my life, by yielding to temptation. I was ready now to "stand."

The baby was born November 18, 1965. The delivery was a very difficult one, but we got through. The baby was fine. I named her Cheryl. The church people helped with food and milk. They wanted us to stay in Brooklyn, but I had to stay on course. I stayed until I was well enough to travel back to Maryland. I had made another detour, but mercy gave me another chance to be what it wanted me to be. I left New York the week before Christmas and went back to Salisbury. The children and the rest of the family were excited and glad to see the baby. They loved her and helped to take care of her.

The circumstances could have prohibited my college education. The professor [Cheryl's father], got married during the month that I had the baby. This was another opportunity to learn how to forgive. For as long as I could remember it had been very difficult for me to forgive. It was hard, but remembering what I had been forgiven of made it much easier to forgive the professor. I used the experience as a milestone to move on from that point. The irony was that his wife and I were scheduled for the same class when I got back to school. This made me more determined to succeed. I studied assiduously and finished my sophomore year with average grades. During that time I went back to my home church and re-dedicated my life to God.

I learned what walking by faith really meant. I

continued to work and go to school. I had a part-time job and the going got rough at times. I had very little money and at times the food supply was short, but our needs were met each day. My mind was made up to serve the Lord with all my spirit, soul, and body. No matter what happened, I would not go back out into where I was. I began to pray more and actively engage in the activities of our church. I went to meetings and as many services as I could during the week. I also spent much time in the library at school. Caring for my family and attending college kept me on the go. I had to trust and use my faith all the way.

I had so many bills that I began to worry and have insomnia. I sought God's help even more and He led me to read Psalm 40. The psalmist wrote, "I waited patiently for the Lord and He inclined unto me and heard my cry." (Psalm 40:1) I read this psalm until I got the rest and peace that was needed. I began to pay off my bills one at a time. At one time my lights, gas, water and telephone were cut off. I took three of my children and walked down to the offices of each of those companies; we touched the outside of the buildings and asked the father to re-connect everything. He answered our prayers; within a month, my lights, gas, water and telephone were all on.   It was a lesson in obedience and faith.

Another time during the winter, I came home from school and found the house cold. We had oil, but the furnace was off. I pushed the starter several times, but nothing happened. I began to pray. As I prayed, I heard a still small voice say, "Play the record, *My God Can Do Anything But Fail*." At first I thought, this is crazy, play a record! Then I thought, I'll try anything, as cold as it is in here now. I put the record on the record player, pushed the starter on the furnace. It started! This happened several times thereafter, and each time, the furnace started when I played that record. My children just laughed. They thought it was the funniest thing they had ever heard of. However by this time they knew that someone was working miracles for us. I told them God knew I did not have money to pay a service man to start the furnace. He wanted us to know that He would never fail. We were experiencing His miracle working power. There is nothing too hard for God. Nothing too strange or unusual for Him to perform.

We ran out of oil quite often at night and had to wait until morning to call the oil company. We slept with blankets and coats piled on the beds. None of us got seriously ill. We were indeed children of destiny.

We lived at 663 Fitzwater Street in Salisbury. There was something so special about that house. My life was saved and many miracles happened there. One particular event occurred when I got behind on the house payments. I was buying the house from Mr. Raymond Weisner, a very prominent real estate broker. He was an elderly gentleman, a devout Catholic, who cared about people. He was always concerned about whether or not I would be able to keep the house, see he knew about my relationship with Fats.

This time he had come to see why I had not paid my payments. I was studying for a test when he arrived. I told him that I did not have the money. He said, "Well, I can't put you and these children out, even though you are three months behind. I tell you what, since you are trying to improve your status by going to college, pay me when you get enough to pay me without using food money, and buy the things you need for the children. Incidentally, have you paid for tuition and bought books for the second semester?" I answered, "No sir, I don't have the money yet." He asked, "How much do you need?" I replied, "About $250.00." He then wrote a promissory note for $250, handed it to me and said, "Go down to First National Bank, sign it, and they will give you the money. You will not have to pay it back until you graduate and get your first job." At that time that was a lot of money.

I thanked God and Mr. Weisner at the same time. I got the money and did not pay a house payment for the next six months because I did not have enough to buy food, clothes and house payments too. Through it all I learned that God is able to see us through the hard times. I walked by faith and my how He, supplied all that we "NEEDED," not wanted.

~A Test Of
Integrity~

CHAPTER 12

The dictionary defines integrity as the state of being complete or whole; uprightness; virtue; soundness or honesty. I heard a story that implies we're better at integrity when we are young. As the story goes, a salesman came to the door and a little boy's mom told him to tell the man she was in the bath tub. The little boy went to the door and told the salesman, "We ain't got no bath tub, but momma told me to tell you she's in it." My grandmother Lot had another word for it. She called it "gumption," which means initiative or spunk. I had to use a lot of old fashioned gumption during the next two years of college.

I paid part of the tuition and was given a Maryland Teachers grant. The grant meant that I either had to pay it back or teach in the state for two years after I graduated. The school was only thirteen miles from my home, but I did not have a car. I hitchhiked to and from school daily. There were many students, teachers, and office workers who went to the college from Salisbury. It was easy to get a ride, but I had to get up about 5:30-6:00 AM. I prepared breakfast, packed lunches for the children, woke them up and gave special instructions to Julia, Ronnie and Karen. Then I walked about six blocks downtown to catch a ride. Thank God someone picked me up five days a week.

Not only did I hitchhike, I also had a brother and two sisters who were in college there at the same time. We all hitchhiked. This is another aspect of my testimony. Our parents did not finish high school, but five of their children graduated from the University of Maryland Eastern Shore. Billy became a Pastor in New York. This is very unique because we were the only children, on my fathers or mothers side that is, of their brothers or sisters children to finish college. It took integrity.

I made the honor roll during my junior and senior years. I did student teaching at Delmar High in Delaware. There were three of us from Princess Anne. We were the first black student teachers at Delmar. We made the front page of the local newspaper. I received an A+ grade in student teaching and a 4.0 in my major the last year.

I graduated on June 1, 1969, with a B.A. in Social Science. It was the culmination of persistence and *gumption* that my grandmother had talked about. As I walked across the platform to receive my degree, every ounce of strength in me wanted to shout out loud, *"Hallelujah! Thank you Jesus!"* I did not want to interrupt the program. I went back to my seat and cried. Then as I watched my classmates receive their degrees, my heart was overjoyed. This was a precious moment for me. I prayed when I got home and thanked God for bringing me out.

My children were extremely happy for their mom's graduation. We had a great celebration. My family, especially my mother was glad. We all rejoiced.

The "real test of integrity" came when I applied for a job as a teacher in my home town. I had borrowed money from the state on the Maryland Teachers Grant, so, instead of paying it back I wanted to teach in the state. A job at home would have made it easier for me to work and be with my family. I needed to be with them because I was a single parent. I soon learned that this was not going to be easy.

I was astonished when I found out how cruel our society can be to its members. I applied for a job in Wicomico County, the county where I was born, went to elementary school and high school, and had lived for thirty-six years. I was called in for an interview. The interviewer turned me down flat, even though he said that my application was the best that he had seen in quite a while. He said that he could not hire me because I had children and was not married. I was told, and I quote, "the teaching profession is a respectable profession, and we just couldn't allow your morals to degrade it." It was believed that my life would hurt the children and community. I could not believe what I had heard. He said, I probably would not be hired anywhere on the eastern shore. I thanked the man for calling me down to his office and left with tears streaming down my face. I knew that I had been forgiven of my past. My integrity and faith was being tested.

I went home, cried and prayed asking for help to forgive the interviewer. I had told the truth. He asked if I had been divorced. When I told him that I had never been married, he treated me like a tramp from skid row. Throughout the entire ordeal I remembered that my faith had never failed me. I was sure that I would still get a job teaching school because I was ready.

I continued to apply for a job in the state of Maryland. After about a month I received a telegram from Anne Arundel County, Annapolis, Maryland. There was an offer for a position teaching tenth grade World History. This was the subject I liked best. The job was at Southern Senior High in Harwood, Maryland, in the southern part of Anne Arundel County, a rural district. I knew that this was God's divine will for me. I had been born and raised in a rural area. I accepted the offer, however, that meant that I would have to make a definite sacrifice. The job would take me from my children and my family in Salisbury.

I prayed about how to handle the situation. I did not have money or faith enough to take the children with me. I decided to move out of the home and let the children stay with my parents since they were already scheduled for school in Salisbury. I planned to come home every two weeks and send money for their upkeep. Julia was old enough to help mom. I discussed it with mom, and then made the final preparations. This was one of the hardest decisions that I had ever made. It was extremely difficult to leave my children and the home we had lived in for so many years. So the children and I moved out of the home and I took a job 110 miles away.

I went to Annapolis for my interview. The personnel manager was very nice and everything went well. I had the job. I went back home and made the necessary preparations for my children.

I went back to Annapolis via Trail-Ways the first day of school. I did not know where I would stay that night or how I would get to school daily. I got a taxi from the bus station to the school which was about 15 miles out of the city. The fare was twelve dollars, but the man charged ten after I told him that I had traveled from the Eastern Shore that morning. He couldn't believe that I had traveled that far to work at Southern Senior. I knew that things would work together for my good. By the end of the day, one of the teachers had found a room and transportation for me. The room was downtown Annapolis on Lafayette avenue. One of the teachers lived about ten blocks there and offered to give me a ride for a small monthly charge. I was all set. This was a real challenge. I looked forward to my new role of school teacher.

The interview with the Board of Education in Salisbury left scars. I did not tell anyone about my family when I got to the school. The other teachers talked about their children, but I just listened. I felt inhibited and really wanted to tell them about my sweet children, about Julia helping to care for her brothers and sisters. I had a fear of being talked about and hurt. The only thing that kept me going was the knowledge that I loved my children and had learned to love myself more now, than ever. I knew that my parents, brothers and sisters loved us and I would be back home in two years. My heart was encouraged each time I thought about how far faith had brought me.

The first week of school was hectic. The classes were adjusting; students were excited and some were not too happy to return. I put my foot down with those tenth graders the first day. One of the students tested my will power by telling me that I had taken the place of a teacher who had a nervous breakdown the year before. My reply was, *"Oh, I am sorry about Mr. X, but I am here to stay. I do not plan to be sick or absent for any reason this entire year. Aren't you glad?"* My, was he astounded. Before the year was out I had gained the reputation of *"the teacher who never gets sick."* When the year ended, I had received a very favorable rating by our supervisor. I enjoyed my role as a school teacher. I taught at Southern Senior for two years.

During the summer of the third year a door opened near my home. I got a job in the state of Delaware, at Sea Ford Senior High about 21 miles from home. They had interviewed me before I graduated, but I could not work out of the state of Maryland for two years. I could now work and stay at home with my family. I could leave home at 7:00 AM, be on the job by 7:45 AM and return home in the evening. Three teachers, who worked in Seaford and lived in Salisbury, and I were able to join the riding pool. This turned out to be the best position that I had ever had. I loved the school and the students. I was at peace in my spirit. I could now buy the things for the children and be with them at home. I could attend my home church. With all my faith and patience, it worked together for good. Everything was not perfect but I was so happy to be with my family. Love makes a home. I was now ready to embrace what was ahead for our lives.

After a period of time, I went to pay Mr. Weisner, my landlord, back. I made a plan to take a cab to his office after my first job was more settled. That's what I did. I saved enough money to cover both the promissory note as well as the past due rent. When I arrived at his office there were a few customers ahead of me so I waited for him. Soon I was greeted by Mr. Weisner with a huge smile and a big *"You did it!"* along with a sobering embrace. My eyes began to fill with tears that I was able to fight back as I went into my purse to get the envelope that had the money in it. I said with a smile, "Here you are sir, every dollar, you can count it sir", I said so proudly. He took the envelope from my hand, looked at it for a quick few seconds and said *"Thank you Virginia,"* graciously, *"But,"* he said slowly and quietly as he gently reached out to take my hand, folding the envelope into it, *"Keep this and use it for the children."* I was speechless as I walked down the steps of his office in resounding joy, disbelief, and tear soaked cheeks.

THE END….(?)

PART THREE

A LITTLE MORE

~There's a little more
to the story~
Karen Domino White

CHAPTER 13

After years of traveling on the road with Fats
and being cared for, my mother worked hard and
was finally able, through some very rough times
and dedication, to earn her college degree, with
honors. She continued on to her passion of
becoming a high school teacher specializing in
Black History, which she loved. Later, while still
teaching at another school in Seaford, Delaware,
she was appointed to start the first gospel choir at
Seaford Senior High, which helped to fulfill her
musical appetite.

In 1977, while working in a church ministry,

my mother met Ted Byrd through a mutual friend. After being a single working woman with strong change in her personal dedication to her faith, my mother married Ted. Sometime after ending her teaching position she made the decision to become an ordained minister. They traveled the country together as evangelistic ministers and remained married until Ted departed this life in the late 1990's.

Years had gone by with little or no communication between my mom and my dad except through my brothers and me. In early 2001 my mom became ill and my dad was concerned with her wellbeing. He decided he wanted to help. So a few days later he sent her a substantial amount of money in the form of a several money orders. He felt he needed a go between so he sent them to my address and I sent them on to her. He wanted to contact her personally, but was still a little nervous because of all the years that had gone by. I assured him that it was okay to call her and he did. They spoke briefly. That conversation will always be between the two of them, forever. My mother departed this life in November of 2001.

After several decades of being apart from mom I soon discovered a "huge epiphany." My father was never, ever able to get over the rejection from my mother! She constantly turned down his marriage proposals, too many times to mention. He was devastated for years! No one had ever turned my dad down in this manner. Fats Domino had become an icon at this level in the music business, so getting turned down was very rare for him. In the early nineties, my dad had a performance at the Valley Forge Music Fair, in Pennsylvania and I attended. After a fantastic show, I waited for him to change and we met down in an exclusive bar. By now we had begun to have and maintain a good relationship so our conversation was beautiful. During our conversation my dad expressed to me, "I really don't understand why your mom wouldn't come with me".....Do you know why?" I questioned, "What do you mean?" He said, "I really loved her and I wanted her to be with me." I was pleasingly stunned by this declaration, since I had never heard my dad make any such intimate statements about mom. He's basically a man who does not express his most personal feelings openly. By the same token, I knew they had a bond much stronger than a "soul tie." Ultimately, when I responded I said, "Well, what did you expect, you had a fam....." but he cut me off by saying "no but I was gonna' be with her, I just don't know why." as he sulked in a most vulnerable way. I had never seen him so broken. So I tried to get him out of that mental space by saying, "Well you two, as a couple, were only together for what 10 years?" To which he abruptly, forcefully said "10 years?!?!"...It was more like 20!! *WOW*, I said to myself, this was even deeper than I realized because they met in 1954 and here it was 1990!! And here he was "clearly" re-living this as if it were *YESTERDAY!* This was amazing to me.....my dad never healed from the rejection, or anger. He was very, very, angry about the breakup and the way mom left him. Like I said, he never got over it and in many ways neither did my mom. They both shut down inside. Shut down emotionally, internally, and mentally. Definitely an "Epiphany."

My mom began writing her story in 1984. It was her strong desire to encourage young women, as well as men, to love and care for themselves first and to move aggressively through whatever their own personal circumstances and challenges. By seeking help whenever needed will allow them to move towards their main purposes, passions and dreams.

With hard work and dedication, my mom did it as a single parent with five children.... you can too. Always remember to dedicate yourselves to strong faith and belief in God, first and foremost.

A view of the beginning of the property.

In the mid 80's, unfortunately the home

purchased by my father, Fats, as destroyed by a horrible fire. While no one was residing in the dwelling, an array of memorabilia and pictures were gone forever. *EVERYTHING* my siblings and I owned in that home was destroyed. To this day we still own the property *(though we have had many sale offers).*

Location of the property.

Every time I visit the corner lot of the property, I get excited knowing that it has its own Private Place in History....you know like "this is where it all went down," "back in the day"... *"THE DOMINO AFFECT"*....

To this day my father, Fats Domino, resides in New Orleans, Louisiana.

A Few Insights

By

Karen Domino White

~*The Onion*~

<u>Insight 1</u>

Life is an interesting animal. Meaning it can go from being tame to being a beast, in a relatively short period of time. Predictable, yet not. Does anyone have all the pieces to the puzzle? You do know that's what life is, right? A huge puzzle, broken up into one million, trillion pieces. Realize, there's one thing about it......life is real. Many of us have a challenge that is somewhat innate......peeling off the layers, you know, the *onion thang*.

In conversation with many people, generally, I have come to notice the first layer is the hardest to shed. That's the cover layer. Thin, but hard to get loose. That's the layer that begins to reveal, usually, what we don't want people to see. Oh how it hurts!!!

Most of us know the story. Ever since the Garden of Eden, guess what, "The biggest cover up ever!" Yep, "Who told you that you were naked?" What makes us think that a fig leaf will hide the real issues? Issues? Yeah we all have them. Small, medium, large, x-large, xx-large, xxx-large, and but of course, supersized, never the less, ISSUES! The fear of being revealed is a horrific emotional state to find ourselves in. Sadly, so many times we don't even know why we are the way we are. You can become paralyzed by fear, yet most things that we become fearful about, never come to pass. No wonder, some have described the very word fear as;

*F*alse
*E*vidence
*A*ppearing
*R*eal

So true. The mind is very powerful, and most of the things we fear never come to pass. Having said all of this, personally, I want to share my perspective on life and some of my experiences with my mom and dad.

When we were kids we lived for the moment. While we are growing into our different phases, we were oblivious to the real circumstances and challenges surrounding the very ones who brought us in this world, our parents. And don't think for a minute they're gonna' tell you what you wanna' know, "NOT GONNA HAPPEN!" Well at least you can rest assured you won't get the full story, it's way too painful for some and some things really are traumatic. I'm basically referring to general, everyday things that have happened to our parents as they were growing up. We as children, never think about the things that have happened in their lives that made them the way they are, and for the most part, their onion has never been peeled……Nor has the puzzle been solved.

~I'm Here Because...~

Insight 2

I'm Karen. I'm one of Fats Domino's daughter's. I have two brothers, Veron and Anton. I'm probably the most outspoken one of the three, and yes, Fats Domino....He's our father. In Ebony Magazine, May 1974, there was an article about my dad. It talks about his lifestyle, his diamond jewelry, accomplishments, how he had gambled away two million dollars without going broke, etc. A little further down in the article, it talks about his family and it is stated something like this; children, eight and (3). Yeah...us. Eight children at home and (3) at the other place he called home, in Maryland (at the time), with my (our) mother. Of course this really isn't a big deal. I'm just stating facts. The facts matter. It has been "alleged" that there are even a few more siblings…..Shocked? Please don't be….Thus this chapter entitled, *"I'm here because."*

I've read a couple of articles on my dad. The frustrated writers had one common thread……It was that no one could ever get any specifics on my dad's personal life. You know, *"the dirt."* They would say things like, "I know he's had some "issues" in his relationship, (his marriage at home), he liked to drink, and he was unfaithful. By the way, did I mention that it has been "alleged" that there are even a few more siblings? So don't be surprised if other stories surface after this one is released.

The reality is that I only know my life. This is my deal…..Our story. Lots of times when you are the child of an entertainer, you really don't think about it as others do. As a matter of fact, often we don't even have the whole picture until later on in our lives when we start asking our own questions and or do our own searching. I was so very fortunate and blessed in 2010, at the Rock-n-Roll Hall of Fame in Cleveland Ohio, to meet a very good friend of my dad's. It was none other than, "Mr. Billy Diamond." He was, at the time, in his 90's. Having lived so long, I found him to be most fascinating, and boy did he drop a wealth of knowledge on me. Remarkable memory! He without hesitation, let me know that he was the best manager that my dad ever had. Great sense of humor! Never knew that just shy of year later, we would lose him at the age of 95. What a man. Among many things, he let me know how well he knew mom and how highly respected she was, within the circle of friends, and most notably, how important my mother was to my dad. The fame and material things, indeed, tend to be the focus as we look in from the outside. No surprise that it was not the reality of how things really were. Don't get it twisted. There's always a deeper meaning.

~*SECRETS?*~

Insight 3

Tyler Perry ......Call Me!

This is why I love Tyler Perry's movies so...so much. "Thanks Tyler." What we think is a hidden thing, never is. Mr. Perry always has a killer surprise, especially at the dinner table. The so called, "family secret." It's just awesome! The characters can never point the finger because no one is totally clean from anything! I may have mentioned this before, but if just "ONE" other person knows something that we have deemed to be unknown to everyone else that we know...... then...... there's no secret......no such animal.

First of all, if you've been on this earth long enough to observe life, you know that people are people and there are lots of things that make us do what we do. If there's a secret to be told, eventually, someone's gonna tell. We're not that good at holding things in. How many of us have shared something personal with a really close friend. A little time goes by and everything seems to be still cool. You haven't heard any repercussions. Five years go by, six, and seven ......and then one day you're talking to another friend and lo and behold a small piece, not the whole thing, slips out of the corner of their lips that "they heard from so and so........." What????!!!! But I thought .... yeah you did ...... Like I said, there are NO SECRETS!....

~Put the puzzle together Or Peel the onion?~

Insight 4

Where should I start? Well in *Insight 1*, I mentioned an onion that had never been peeled. And which one would you rather be?

Since I was conceived by my mom and dad, I've surrendered to the fact that this is how it was supposed to be. If you were to ask my two brothers, I'm sure you would get uniquely different points of view that all lead to the same destination…We are here.

Sooooo…………Who's idea was this? How did this happen, you may have asked yourself periodically. We spend time coming up with reasons and questions why we become so devastatingly scattered as adults, or become riveted with so many things that we clearly did not ask for. Think about the wild ways and vast differences in the ways that we humans react to simple things in our lives. Given the same situation one person could blow up shouting out long streaming line of profanities, while another will become a total introvert. Why? Something happened along the way of living. Besides the fact that everyone is born with their own natural predisposition to be a certain way, something really happens along the way of living. How do you begin to pull the whole thing together? Remember, you have an onion and a puzzle which both consist of lots of pieces. They have a central characteristic. They are both carriers of an ability to provoke a type of pain, emotional or mental, which releases a physical reaction. Keep in mind that all pain is not bad.   Take the onion. The first thing that happens almost as soon as the first layer of outer skin is peeled off is the body's normal defense, tears. Do you know why? Onions contain a component called the "lachrymatory factor," from the Latin word "lacrima" or tear. Who knew that just the simple process of removing a layer of an onion, would cause such a drastic reaction in the human body. Funny thing about it is, the crying reaction only lasts as long as the onion is being peeled. Interesting, right? As you peel and peel, it hurts and stings more and more and the tears multiply. There are not many vegetables, other than eating hot peppers that naturally, without provocation, brings a human being to instant tears like the onion. You don't even have to bite the onion. Just start to undress it, as if to expose it!

As we know, there are several varieties of onions. The layers are tighter and even more intertwined, the deeper you go into an onion. Most of our human layers are pretty much the same. The differences vary depending on the measures of each issue individuals have received. So, I may have received a lot more guilt and you may have received a lot more rejection, and so forth.

Now we have the puzzle, because life tends to consist of scattered pieces. Millions of them! Starting to put it together can be the most intense part. You've got the puzzle in a huge box and it needs to be all dumped out on the table or floor. The important point is it all has to be placed out together for all to see. Here we are, no place to hide. Once again, total exposure. Now is the time to find that first piece. Pick up one piece...well it looks like the right one. . .okay, next. Oh it's too round. Darn it! The next piece has that crazy angle and a point on the end. So I guess I'll take the onion for 300, please. . . . . Seeeeeee?

They both can be excruciating, but we have to make a choice. If you choose to live the rest of your life in denial, it will become a travesty because all the pieces in our lives want to be found. I believe that it's not that we are going to find "ALL" of them, but we have to let the process begin in order to start becoming whole! No one person can carry lifelong baggage. Sooner or later those suitcases burst. Overloading and stuffing ourselves with guilt, hurt, anger, and shame is extremely unhealthy for the body, spirit, and soul. We were not meant to be dumping stations! The issue with the puzzle is that the first piece that you pick up may not be what you thought it was. You thought Aunt Mary was your aunt until Uncle John spits out by mistake one day, at a family get together no less, that she's your…. What?… MOM? Yeah, life is wild,… just like that. How about the families where all the children grew up in the same house with the same two parents. One day someone comes to the door and ask to see so and so, who you have always known as your sister or brother, with the same parents you've all known for years. This person says, "Hi, I'm so and so's dad. . . What! These crazy things happen, every day, often times, at the detriment of unsuspecting young and older victims who are often times left to fend for themselves. Why do we do these things to one another? Many a broken human spirit in this world, has been left in a pocket of hurt and turmoil with no immediate answers. My heart cries for honesty to prevail. By the way,…. I choose the onion. Peel and heal. And THE CYCLE CONTINUES ………… Story?. . .Everybody has one. Joy, Peace, and Love is my hope and dream for you. Please Live, so you can come alive…..*Karen*

Conclusion

When we are young, we lived as young people do. As life goes on so do we. No one has ever had the manual on how to do it right. There is no such document. Whatever road we take is our road... you can't walk mine and I can't walk yours, nevertheless, we must walk. Just remember that nothing is ever the mistake that we sometimes may think that it is when it's happening. Without things happening... there would be... no journey. Stuff is going to happen. We can't change what we can't change. Hear, *as well as can be expected,* the still small voice inside and walk by faith. You are more than valuable and there is a "*Majestic*" purpose for your life, thus the reason you are here. By the way, on your way through your life, learn to kick fear, shame, and insecurity completely down by building yourself up with your powerful faith!! We all have been given a measure of faith and as we look, pray, and ask for guidance, let go and surrender our innermost selves, our best lives are still ahead. ***There is nothing to fear once faith has taken control!***

Letters
To
<u>*Mom*</u>

~Mom asked us to write these letters that
she include in her book~

March 7, 1985
Something About My Mother
By Karen V. White

Looking back on my early-years, there are several things that I could dwell on when it comes to my upbringing. The thing I remember most about my mother is her spiritual steadfastness. I never understood why my mother prayed so much. We lived in a rather old house. Once a week my mom would invite a few women over. They would have something they called a prayer meeting. As I said earlier we had an old house and boy! When they began to pray it seemed like the whole house would shake to no end. Wow! Was I embarrassed! All of my friends would be outside playing and my brothers and I were inside this old dancing, brown house on the corner, I just hated it! The thing is that everyone knew us! I had an image to maintain! Especially in my high school years (smiles).

My mother was very prudent. For example, my youngest brother had a habit of sneaking out of the house and putting pillows in his place as if he were in bed. Well, I always knew when he was in for it. About 12:00 or so mom would wait for him to come in, go upstairs and get at least in his first stage of sleep, you know, nice and drowsy. A few minutes' later wham, wham, wham. Needless to say my brother was no longer asleep. She would let him have it, right in his sleep. What a nightmare!

When I was out of high school, the first summer I went out with my friends as most teenagers do. Financially we were not stable. My mother had raised five children alone; worked and graduated from College. Every time I would ask my mom for money, even if it were one dollar, she gave it; I would be on my way out to the local club. I can't remember wanting for anything that I needed. Somehow the Lord always made, always made a way, always!! If anything was wrong mom would usually just say, "Let's pray about it, the Lord will make a way somehow."

I remember once when our phone bill was past due. Mom said to us kids, "Come on, we're going to walk downtown to the phone company." Pretty normal right? Wrong! The phone company was closed. My mother had every intention of walking around that phone company, actually putting our hands on the building and praying. Talk about stress! I just knew that all of my friends would see me, and say what in the world are those nuts doing now? Of course no one saw us, but being ignorant of the word of God, I just thought the craziest things. But as you might have guessed, the Lord miraculously made a way for us to keep our telephone. I later learned that my mother had done this out of obedience to the Lord, as an act of faith.

I could go on and on, but the fondest memories of my childhood come in the biblical verses. "Train up a child in the way he should go and when he is old, he will not depart from it." Praise the Lord] That is so true in my life. I thank God for a wonderful husband and three beautiful children. I find myself doing some of the same things that my mother used to do and teach us. Even though my children are young, I've already seen some of the positive results of living for God and knowing who you are in Jesus Christ. The Lord has brought us a long way. Praise God! I love you mom!

My Mother
March 30, 1985
By: Daughter Julia

I have fond memories of my mother and family as a child. We were brought up in a Christian household and I feel that makes a world of difference in raising children to adults.

We were a close knit family and we still are. As the sole provider, for herself and five children, I think I can best describe my mother as strong willed and a survivor and a truly beautiful person. We had our hard times and setbacks, but they were normal.

As the oldest of five children and a female, we had our little mother daughter differences, But I will admit that as far as discipline is concerned, she was kind of fair and open-minded which I can only appreciate now as an adult, and a mother, better than when I was younger, (smile)

I will always remember our special family gatherings such as Thanksgiving and Christmas, etc. They were always fun except for dishwashing afterwards.

One of my most valued memories of our mother is that while raising us, she studied for and obtained a Bachelor's Degree. Receiving a degree is a reward in itself, but I think the fact that she obtained hers while raising a family deserves a little extra credit.

I think we have a nice, well rounded family group and at this point I don't think I would trade them for any other.

My positive and treasured family memories are so numerous that I think I could go on and on, but not to brag, I am very fortunate to have a solid family background, I have to give the majority of the credit to my mother, especially to her inner strength and attitude towards raising children.

Mom
April, 1985
By: Daughter Cheryl

Although my mother possesses many qualities, there are three that I admire most. Her undying faith and trust in God; her love for her children and her humility. Qualities I would like to have as I mature.

This faith and trust in God that I mentioned comes from her personal relationship with God. When I was a child and living in Maryland, I remember mom telling us, the kids, to come down stairs to pray. Mom didn't seem to care what time it was; if we had needs she would just pray as if prayer was the only way our needs would be met. Now I know, I began to find this out when after prayer, we lacked nothing. I know that this God we were talking to really is the source of all my supply. I am very thankful that this person whom mom trusted so dearly, God did not let her down, for it is because of God proving Himself to mom that I now have my faith and trust in Him.

Even though mom had faith and trust in God, if she had not had so much love for my brothers, sisters and me, I may have disregarded or at least tried to, all that faith and trust business.

I remember getting lots of Christmas gifts. Mom would buy toys for all of us and nothing for herself. I remember her buying me new shoes and clothes, while she may have had only about two pair of shoes, for herself.

Although mom was a single parent, who worked hard to support us, she never seemed too busy to read stories to me, or answer questions I had. Now that I am older, this still holds true. Mom is even more understanding and loving. I can say today that my mom is my closet friend on this earth.

It takes a humble person, not a weak one to follow, when she's used to leading. Mom was a single parent until she was 44 years old. God blessed her to learn humility through much suffering. I love you mom.

My Mother
July 15, 1985
By: You're Loving Son, who loves you,
Veron A. Polk (Ronnie)

There are many things and many years to, express the way I feel about this very special lady, so I would like to start from the time that I was a little boy. I was just old enough to realize what life was about. Mom was the type to realize that fact, she then began to show me the rights and wrongs of my life. My childhood was a very happy one. There were times when mom didn't know if we were going to make it through the next night, so we would all get together, my two sisters and my brother and pray. Mom would always make sure that all her children were close to the Lord.

Since I was oldest son, I traveled with mom a

lot. I remember going from house to house praying for the sick and elderly. I would always carry the bible and pray by her side. Mom was always respected where ever she went. She was remembered as the woman who preached so well and turned out most churches. Mom worked real hard to make sure we had the things we needed, even, when times were the toughest.

When I was going through school mom always mate sure that whatever I did, school came first. She would help me with all my problems no matter what they were (even getting my hair cut for the school pictures),

My mother is a very warm and loving person. One who tries to help those who need help. She taught me the meaning of life, a meaning that I will never forget.

As far as mothers go, I don't think a son could find one any better than mine. My feelings for you mom are much too much to write down, on paper, but in my heart there will never be a stronger love than the love have for you, because no matter how far away you are, I want you to remember I love you very, very much.

MY MOM

Mom you are the vision of strength that I shall always look upon. From the very first day, I was able to realize who and what you are. I know God is your strength. Many times we went through hard times and each time God brought us through. Somehow we are able to come through those tough times and still be healthy normal kids, with no criminal records or long jail sentences, like the kids in our neighborhood were going through during those years.

I love you very much and words cannot really express the godliness and good works you showed all of us. Your life has been a good example. I wish I could do a little to have all mothers follow your lead.

Now that I have grown up, I look back and realize I made many mistakes. Those things I cannot change. You taught me to look into those mistakes and make them work to my advantage. The greatest blessing was the ability to stick to our bible background and live it out in our daily lives. Nothing could be more valuable with each passing day. I still think of you often. I'm glad you have chosen to follow the road to heaven and placed God first and foremost in our minds.

Today I feel I'm a better man because of the strength of my mother. Although our roads have not crossed recently, I know within you some goodness will be passed on to those you meet in your travels.

As I sit here and write to you, I realize these words only catch a glimpse of your actual deeds. I would never be able to put them all down on paper. I want to thank you for being a super mom, a child of God and my best friend. There is so much I want to say, but most of all, it's that I love you very much and that you are the best mom anyone could ever have.

Love,
Anton

Inspiring Words

from

Virginia Byrd

EPILOGUE

The Lord has inspired me to write this book for His glory. I pray that it will be a blessing to those who are without hope. May the anointing of the Holy Ghost draw you to God.

I was lost in a dark world of rebellion, fear, unbelief, unforgiveness, torment, pride, hatred and insecurity, but I came to myself, just as the prodigal son did. The bible says, "And when he came to himself, he said, "How many hired servants of my father's have bread enough and to spare, and I perish with hunger!" I will ARISE and GO to my father and will say unto him, Father, I have sinned against heaven, and before thee," (St. Luke 15:17-18). I no longer desired to continue on the broad road to destruction. I sought the Lord and found the answer one day -as I heard Him say to me, "I am the way, the truth and the life, no man cometh unto the Father, but by me."(John 14:6).

We are now living in an era of social and

religious groups. Teenage suicide is up, abortion, divorce, child abuse, illegitimacy, sexual perversion, and social diseases such as Aids and Herpes are all rampant in the land. The devil is on the loose. The bible says, "This know also that in the last days perilous times shall come." These are the perilous times spoken of in II Timothy, Chapter 3. God said, "If my people which are called by my name, shall humble themselves, and pray and seek my face, and turn from their wicked ways; then will I hear from heaven, and will forgive their sin, and will heal their land." (II Chronicles 7:14).

There are thousands of men, women, boys and girls caught up in the tide of sin. Many despondent teenagers, unwed mothers, alcoholics, drug addicts, unsubmissive wives, and unfaithful husbands have found themselves in the same predicament that I found myself in. They too, are searching for answers, but have not found the way out of their dilemmas.

My friend, if this is your plight now; I want

you to know that there is a way out. It is through Jesus Christ. He is, waiting for you to take a bold step. Open the door to a more abundant life. He says to you, "Behold I stand at the door and knock: If any man hears my voice and opens the door, I will come in to him, and will sup with him and he with Me." (Revelations 3:20).

God is a God of abundance. Abundance of love, forgiveness, finances and life. He has everything you need. This is His promise to you, "The thief cometh not, but for to steal, and to kill, and to destroy: I am come that they might have life, and that they might have it more abundantly." (St. John 10:10). Yield to Jesus and enjoy an abundance of life. An abundance of spiritual, physical and financial prosperity. He is ready and willing to heal your whole spirit, soul and body.

Satan's trick is to keep you from turning your life over to God. He tells you that you're a nobody, or you've gone too far and God has forsaken you. My friend that is a lie. God loves you more than you love yourself. If you fail Him, He still remains faithful. He is a friend that sticketh closer than a brother. "Greater love has no man than this that a man lay down his life for his friends." (St. John 15:13).

Perhaps you are a backslider, or have never known God. A good way to start is to be honest. The scripture says, "If we confess our sins, He is faithful and just to forgive us our sins and to cleanse us from ALL unrighteousness." (I John 1:9). There is no sin too big or too small for God to forgive.

Ask forgiveness. Repent of your sins. You will find God right there, still loving you.

Dear friend, eternal life is your most important business today. Tomorrow may be too late. If you do not have this assurance, pray this prayer with me now-—Lord Jesus, I confess that I am a sinner and I ask you to forgive me. I believe in my heart that you are the Son of God and that He raised you from the dead. I now accept you as my Lord and

Savior. Thank you Lord, for saving me. In Jesus'
Dear name, Amen.

You are free! "There is therefore now no
condemnation to them which are in Christ Jesus,
who walk not after the flesh, but after, the Spirit."
(Romans 8:1), "If the Son therefore shall set you
free, you shall be free indeed." (St. John 8:36).
Now live for God.

PHOTO LIBRARY

Our Extraordinary Mother

Virginia Byrd

Karen's first time meeting Mrs. Domino in 1996

Karen and her dad, Fats Domino

Veron and his dad, Fats Domino, in Atlantic City circa 1987

Fats Domino surrounded by his children
Karen, Veron, and Anton

Fats Domino's son, Anton (now)

Karen and her dad, Fats Domino, and her husband Maurice

Karen's firstborn son, Soyica with his Grandfather,
FAT'S in Atlantic City

Soyica (Karen's firstborn) and his grandfather Fats Domino

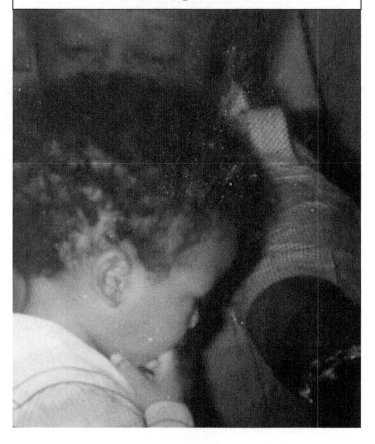

Karen's son Lateef gazing at his grandfather's diamond gold watch

*Karen's son
Lateefius
Maximus III
Artist*

Karen's daughter
Keira
Professional
"Hair Guru"

Karen's granddaughter Imani

Karen at her father's star
~Fats Domino~

***Fats Domino star on Hollywood Walk of Fame
6616 Hollywood Blvd.,***

Karen on the star of her father
~Fats Domino~

Fats Domino with Nat King Cole 1964
*Courtesy saxophonist Herb Hardesty

*Karen and her best friend, Rita Donohue,
a treasure in her life.*

Thankful to one of my mentors, supermodel Pat Cleveland, who has inspired me with her kindness and has taken my ability to think, hope and believe the impossible to its highest level. Thank You!

Karen interviewing CeCe Winans as a Gospel Liason

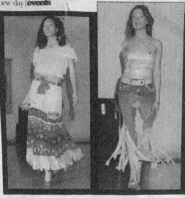

LOVE AFFAIRS
(continued from page 36)

Expect to be in a loving relationship where you can enhance each other's spiritual, growth and development. Don't place your sense of peace and ability to love in the hands of someone who hurt or betrayed you. You are in control of how you relate to people. You are worthy of a trusting relationship. Heal by forgiving and letting go of past hurts, wounds, and pain.■

MAN TALK
(continued from page 23)

no one has to know about what we were doing. But I knew better than to believe that garbage. The people around us might not know and they could get fooled for a time. But God wouldn't get fooled. He sees all.

How was I going to win an argument with Him?■

molested other family members. She had spent the majority of her teen years and young adulthood living the after effects of trauma and depression. When she was finally in a position to begin working with a therapist and start healing, she legally renamed herself. Her father had chosen her name at birth, but she knew she would have to reclaim it if she wanted to move out from under his abusive shadow. Her new name, given to her by God, S.O.L.L.I.A.N., remarkably stands for "She Only Looks Like It Ain't Hurting." The moment she told me, I thought, that could be the middle name of every Black woman I know, and it inspired the title for this book.

Every time I give a talk or a workshop I am almost overwhelmed by the number of sisters I meet who are in pain. Some days I can literally feel the desperation rushing out to me like a solid wave, because it's desperation I myself have lived. (You know this book is "by us for us," but these are experiences that can be every woman's.

the sharing—if you will step outside your safety net—that lets you know that there are millions just like you.

It's our stories that will save our lives. When women see that I'm living through my pain, talking about it openly and without shame, they believe that maybe, just maybe, it's possible for them to do the same. Talking about my pain isn't the hardest part anymore; it's trying to get the women I meet to understand that the beginning of a way to heal our pain lies in our willingness to look at the issues that make up pain's foundation.

In the following pages I'm going to share stories of a particular kind. These stories explore issues that bring many of us the kind of long-term pain that can lead to depression.■

From BLACK PAIN *by Terrie Williams. Copyright © 2007 by Terrie Williams. Reprinted by permission of Scribner, and imprint of Simon & Schuster, Inc.*

*Karen's "Jean Therapy" clothing line as featured in Hype Hair Magazine. *Compliments "New Day Associates"*

A portion of Karen's vocal season

Karen Domino White

Open Our Eyes
featuring
Karen Domino White & Friends

y-nominated artist
ne Jazz Festival

FILE PHOTO

David Jackson, of Ardmore, Pennsylvania, and Karen
Domino White, of Willingboro, perform with the band
Everyday People, a Sly and The Family Stone
band,   ar's Willingboro Jaz
                        he

*A portion of
Karen's
vocal season*

The Wind beneath my Wings....my rock and love of my life,,,my husband, Maurice

In conjunction with being a Vocalist and Artistic Fashionista, Karen is also a full-fledged Zumba Dance Instructor, and now author.

When Destiny calls
.......Answer....
The blood of my father
flows passionately through
my veins.
Therefore my destiny is
constantly pulsing
me forward forevermore.
Born with a plethora of
instinctive, creative gifts.
I must keep the legacy alive.
Although, like any stream,
it flows on a course of its own
...Free and Easy...

Karen Domino-White

Virginia Byrd

Contact Information For Bookings:

Karen Domino-White

thedominoaffect0228@gmail.com

1 (609) 531-8414

NOTES

NOTES

NOTES

NOTES

NOTES

NOTES

Printed in Great Britain
by Amazon

23760131R00155